More of Him, Less of Me

More of Him, Less of Me

My Personal Thoughts, Inspirations, and Meditations on the WEIGH DOWN™ DIET

Jan Christiansen

STARBURST PUBLISHERS®, INC.
Lancaster, Pennsylvania

To schedule author appearances, write:

Author Appearances
Starburst Promotions®
P.O. Box 4123
Lancaster, Pennsylvania 17604

or call (717) 293-0939.

www.starburstpublishers.com

First Printing, January, 1999
ISBN: 1-892016-00-1
Library of Congress Catalog Number 99-88598
Printed in the United States of America

Cover design by Richmond & Williams
Text design and composition by John Reinhardt Book Design

Contents

Introduction

On a routine trip to the doctor, he gave me some bad news: I had diabetes. The good news was that there was a good chance of controlling the disease with *diet* and *exercise*. (I hate those two words!) He also told me that I needed to lose weight—as if I didn't know that! I had been trying to lose my extra 75 pounds for 26 years. I had read every diet book ever printed and bought every piece of exercise equipment ever manufactured. I had cried, tried, and prayed and eventually just quit trying. So, in that office, I faced the biggest challenge of my life—lose weight or suffer the devastating results of progressing diabetes.

The choice was easy—I decided to lose weight. Visiting my local library to check out the diabetic cookbooks, *The Weigh Down Diet* (Doubleday) by Gwen Shamblin caught my eye. It was the large cross on the cover of the book that prompted me look inside. "Maybe God could help me lose weight," I thought. Quickly skimming the pages, I discovered only a few basic guidelines. "Too simple," I told myself, searching for the menu plans, recipes, and exercise guidelines. There were none! As I started to put the book back, something stopped me. "It can't hurt to read it," I thought.

I *devoured* the book! It was so revolutionary, so simple, so hopeful! I learned that Gwen Shamblin had organized Weigh Down Workshops™ that meet all across the country for support and encouragement. I joined one near my home, and the weight began to come off! I lost 35 pounds! I ate exactly what I wanted, I didn't exercise, and most importantly, I got my diabetes under control.

Now I am confident I will continue to lose weight because I have learned to eat the way God intended me to eat. Through Weigh Down™ I learned that I have been in slavery to food, much like the Israelites were in slavery in Egypt. God led them out of Egypt through the desert and into the Promised Land. For me, God has used Weigh Down™ to lead me out of my own personal "Egypt." Now, I'm in what Gwen Shamblin calls the "Desert of Testing." However, it has been a wonderful journey and God has led me each step of the way. I have no doubt that soon I will enter the Promised Land of thinness!

The biggest blessing of my journey has been the tremendous spiritual growth I've experienced. As I applied the Weigh Down™ principles of eating to my life, I began to really seek God. He, in turn, began to open my eyes to wonderful truths in His Word about surrendering my will to Him. He revealed attitudes of my heart and patterns of behavior that had kept me overweight. God even started using humorous circumstances to teach me lessons about self-control.

More of Him, Less of Me is a collection of the sometimes hilarious, sometimes tearful, but always spirit-changing lessons I have learned through the "Desert of Testing." It is not intended to be a replacement for *The Weigh Down Diet*, but a companion book to give you guidance on your journey. I pray that as you share my journey, you will be encouraged and challenged to trust God to help you achieve your proper weight.

If you have given up on losing weight, I urge you to read *The Weigh Down Diet* and join a Weigh Down Workshop™. I know this is God's answer to our cries for help with losing weight. Now, there is hope! You can lose weight and keep it off permanently! Join the thousands of Weigh Down™ participants around the world who make up this great caravan of "Desert Buddies" as we experience success in losing weight. Walk with us as we make our way to the Promised Land. You can do it and God will help!

Your Desert Pal,

Jan Christiansen

http://www.ohiowebsites.com/more/index.html

First Things First

We Begin the Journey

Then they said to him, "Please inquire of God to learn whether our journey will be successful." The priest answered them, "Go in peace. Your journey has the Lord's approval."

JUDGES 18:5-6

There's nothing like a little reassurance right up front for encouragement! When I found this verse at the beginning of my efforts on the Weigh Down™ Diet, my heart leapt for joy. This time I was going to lose weight and this time I was going to keep it off, because this time I was doing it God's way! I had the Lord's approval!

On my journey I was amazed at how quickly the weight came off, but I was even more amazed by the way God stepped right in and began to *help* me lose weight. Every day He would lead me to scripture that spoke directly to my heart. Each time I was tempted to overeat, He would show me a way to overcome the temptation. I could feel God taking every step of this journey with me!

Now, I invite you to come along on my journey to the Promised Land of thinness. Share my ups and downs through the "Desert of Testing." Be encouraged by the scripture that helped me along the way. Laugh with me as God uses his wonderful sense of humor to point me in the right direction.

It doesn't matter whether you are just starting to lose weight or starting over; this time you are going to make it—we will make it together! Traveling is always more fun with a friend, so I'm thrilled to have you for my Desert Buddy!

Today's Tip:

Start a desert journal. Write today's date in it as the first day of your journey, then jot a few notes each day to record your experiences along the way.

The more we appropriate God into our lives the more progress we make on the road of Christian godliness and holiness.
—Madame Jeanne Guyon

God's Work Under Destruction

Do not destroy the work of God for the sake of food!

ROMANS 14:20

This verse stopped me in my tracks one day! I am sure the Lord put it in the Bible just for those of us going through the Weigh Down™ program. I had been struggling as I tried to apply the Weigh Down™ principles to my eating. I decided to dissect the verse.

If I am obedient to God, in the area of eating, what would be the "works of God"?

- I would look better.
- I would feel better both physically and emotionally.
- I would be able to keep my diabetes under control.
- I would have the stamina to participate in athletic activities once again.
- I would be an example to others of God's power to deliver from addiction to food.
- I would enjoy the blessings which result from obedience to God.
- I would be self-controlled in eating which would spill over to other areas of my life.
- I would experience a closer walk with my Lord.
- My faith would be increased to believe God's power to break other strongholds in my life.

Today's Tip:

Write down all the works God can do in your life if you are obedient to Him. Read this list each time you are tempted to eat when not hungry or eat be-

Wow, there are a lot of "works" that God could perform through my obedience in this area. Obedience means eating only when I am hungry and only until I am full. Soooo . . . if I eat when I am not physically hungry or if I eat beyond full, I would be destroying all these wonderful works of God in my life just for the sake of food! I get it, and you know what, it's just not worth it!

There are three stages in the work of God: Impossible; Difficult; Done.
—James Hudson Taylor

Lord, Make Me an Instrument

Do not offer the parts of your body to sin, as instruments of wickedness, but rather offer yourselves to God, as those who have been brought from death to life and offer the parts of your body to Him as instruments of righteousness.

ROMANS 6:13

I love that song "Lord, make me an instrument, an instrument of worship, I lift up my hands in your name. . . ." When I read this verse it reminded me of that song. I started contemplating the different parts of my body which could be used as instruments to glorify God. Here's my own verse on the subject.

Today's Tip:

Submit the members of your body to God and allow Him to make a beautiful song of your life.

Let my hands no longer grab for snacks I do not need,
But let them fold in humble prayer for strength to swallow greed.
My mouth shall not be filled with food morning, noon and night,
But filled with praises for my Lord in whom is my delight.

My ears no longer listen to the food, which calls my name,
For they are ever listening for my God, who does the same.
My feet no more shall wander to the pantry or the fridge,
For they are firmly planted in obedience to Him.

My heart has changed its lover; it no longer beats for food,
But swells with love for Christ, my Lord, so loving and so good.
My life shall be an instrument, played out for all to see,
That God can change the glutton's heart into a symphony.

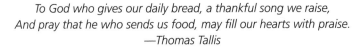

To God who gives our daily bread, a thankful song we raise,
And pray that he who sends us food, may fill our hearts with praise.
—Thomas Tallis

Jesus Knew about Weigh Down™ Principles

Taking the five loaves and two fish and looking up into heaven, He gave thanks and broke the loaves. Then He gave them to His disciples and the disciples gave them to the people. The all ate and were satisfied, and the disciples picked up 12 basketfuls of broken pieces that were left over.

MATTHEW 14:19B-20

Jesus had been preaching and healing all day. Gathered around Him were over five thousand men with their wives and children. Recognizing that the crowd must be experiencing true hunger, (I suspect a large growl) His disciples suggested that Jesus send them all away to get food. But Jesus, knowing there were no fast food drive-thru windows in the area, fed them.

Today's Tip:

Jesus lived His life as an example for us. Follow His example for eating.

Let's examine the methods He used to feed the multitudes:

Jesus looked around for what He had on hand. He was not concerned about calories, fat grams, or exchanges. He took the loaves and fishes, looked up and gave thanks, acknowledging that all food comes from the Father and that we should be thankful for His provision.

He broke the loaves. We are taught to cut our food in half at first to get used to paying attention to the portion sizes we are eating. Soon we are able to judge the correct amount of food to put on our plate, but we must still be careful to stop when satisfied, no matter how much is left.

They all ate and were satisfied. They were not stuffed beyond full, just satisfied. The disciples picked up 12 basketfuls of broken pieces that were left over. Doggie Bags! Carry Outs! These people were definitely NOT members of the "Clean Your Plate Club!" You see, Weigh Down™ principles are not *new*—they are *biblical*. If this way of eating was good enough for Jesus, then surely it's good enough for us!

Spirituality is a way of living; it is also a way of following Jesus.
—Consuelo Del Prado

Whatever

. . . Don't you see that nothing that enters a man from the outside can make him "unclean"? For it doesn't go into his heart but into his stomach, and then out of his body. (In saying this, Jesus declared all foods "clean.")

MARK 7:18B-19

I can eat whatever I want? Can this be true? What about candy, bacon, real butter? Those have always been NO-NO's in the past. What about those "righteous" low-fat, low-calorie, high-fiber foods? Isn't God more pleased with me when I eat only *good* foods? According to this scripture, there are no "good" foods or "bad" foods.

Weigh Down™ teaches us to eat whatever we want. At first the only foods I wanted were all the foods I had been denying myself through years of dieting. I ate lots of cheeseburgers, pizzas, and sweets. But, that soon leveled out, and I began to want a variety of foods. Now I eat an overall balanced diet, even though some days I only want one type of food.

Today's Tip:

Trust the body God created. Trust the Creator!

God's a pretty smart cookie! (Pun intended.) He designed our bodies to know what nutrients it needs, so you can count on it to desire the foods that supply those nutrients. As you are learning to listen for your body to tell you *when* and *how much* to eat, let it also tell you *what* to eat. You should feel free to eat what you are hungry for, even if it is something you previously thought of as bad or fattening.

So, put away all those dieting rules you learned in the past. Take a step of faith and trust that God will lead you in choosing the correct foods. Learn to enjoy all your favorite foods again—but only between the parameters of hungry and full!

He lays upon us no other burden than that of putting our whole trust in Him.
—John Baillie

FIRST THINGS FIRST

Savor the Flavor

...See how my eyes brightened when I tasted a little of this honey.

1 SAMUEL 14:29B

You cannot taste food with your stomach, only with your mouth. This amazing revelation (for me, at least) has been a great help in learning to really enjoy food the proper way.

I always thought I enjoyed good food. What I really enjoyed was eating. I ate very fast, in large quantities, and for many reasons, but I did not really know how to enjoy my food. When you inhale your food, you miss the best part of eating. You miss the delicate hint of cinnamon in a Snickerdoodle, the robust bite of pepper in salsa, or the refreshing sweetness in watermelon. Only the taste buds in your mouth can pick up the fine differences in the flavors of food. Once food has left the mouth and entered the stomach, there is no further taste.

So, slow down, take small bites, and savor the flavor of each food. Don't mix foods in your mouth. It only confuses your taste buds and diminishes the flavor of each individual food.

God could have provided us with all the nutrition we needed in just one food—like manna. We never would have known the difference. But, God meant for us to enjoy our food. That's why He created such a variety of tastes to choose from. Take time to appreciate His creativity and loving provision of a vast array of yummy treats.

Today's Tip:

Eat one of your meals blindfolded, or with your eyes closed as you chew. Notice the unique taste and texture of each food. Savor the flavor! Then thank God for His creativity and kindness toward us.

"The proof of the pudding is in the eating."
—Miguel de Cervantes

He Is Waiting to Be Asked

"Here I am! I stand at the door and knock. If anyone hears my voice and opens the door, I will go in and eat with him, and he with me."

REVELATION 3:20

God wants to help us with every part of our lives—including our eating. He stands knocking at our heart's door. We want His help, but we will not open the door and invite Him to have a meal with us. Why do we expect Him to kick the door down to help us?

That reminds me of the time I attempted to clean my office. It was a mess. Papers, books and dirty cups were everywhere. I had let it go so long, that it was going to take a bulldozer just to get to my desk. How I longed to ask my husband to help me, but I couldn't. It was not his mess; I had done this all by myself, and I would have to clean it all by myself. It's not that he would not have been willing to help me; I was just too embarrassed to ask. Therefore, I struggled through it, and it took me twice the time it would have taken Lee and I to do it together. He would have helped me. Why didn't I ask?

It's the same with my eating. I often struggle through it, making it harder on myself than it needs to be. I don't want to ask God for His help. I figure, I got myself into this, He expects me to get myself out of it. Nothing could be further from the truth! He is standing just outside the door, waiting to be invited to come in and eat with me. And now with Weigh Down™, I know I can't do anything without letting him in.

Today's Tip:

Open the door and invite Him to come in and eat with you. It will make obedience so much easier!

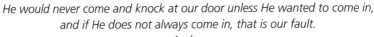

He would never come and knock at our door unless He wanted to come in, and if He does not always come in, that is our fault.
—Ambrose

Oasis

Congratulations! You're on your way to losing weight once and for all. If you are like me, you have dreamed of what it would be like to be thin again. You have probably thought about all the reasons you want to lose weight and all the things you will do once you have lost the weight.

Why not make a list of these things here? That way when the going gets tough, you can refer back to this list and remind yourself of your goals. This has helped me many times when I faltered in my determination to keep going.

Fix these goals firmly in your mind and review them often. They will encourage you to persevere. You will make it!

Praise and Reflection

That . . . ye might be partakers of the divine nature . . .

II Peter 1:4

More Like the Master

More like the Master I would ever be
More of His meekness, more humility
More zeal to labor, more courage to be true
More consecration for work He bids me do
More like the Master I would live and grow
More of His love to others I would show
More self-denial like His in Galilee
More like the Master I long to ever be

CHARLES H. GABRIEL

Reflection

I pray the desire of your heart will be
More of Him and Less of Me!

Blessings & Benefits

Thank You, Lord

Let them give thanks to the Lord for His unfailing love and His wonderful deeds for men, for He satisfies the thirsty and fills the hungry with good things.

PSALM 107:8

It just occurred to me that while half the people in the world are fighting obesity, the other half is fighting starvation! We are so blessed in America to have food in abundance. There's a grocery store or restaurant on every street corner and a garden in most yards. Our government has programs to feed the hungry, and our churches have programs to feed the poor. We have so much food that we can pass out free samples in stores and put more down our garbage disposals in a week than many people see in a month! We are indeed a blessed nation.

How have we handled the abundance? Personally, I have taken it for granted. I've never had to worry about going hungry or thirsty. Though times were lean as I grew up, there was always food on the table. Until I became a Christian, I never took time to be thankful for the food I ate. Although now I bow my head at each meal to ask God's blessing on the food, I don't know that I have ever experienced true thankfulness, because I have never experienced true hunger.

My response to God's abundant provision has been to gorge myself—to eat far more than my portion, to overload my body with food. Now, I find myself fighting to get some of it off. How foolish and ungrateful I've been. God does satisfy the thirsty and fill the hungry, but I am sure He would appreciate a little thanksgiving for the provision.

Today's Tip:

Take time to truly give God thanks for your food and drink, for His unfailing love, and for His wonderful deeds.

We should spend as much time in thanking God for His benefits as we do in asking Him for them.
—Vincent de Paul

He Will Bless Our Food and Heal Our Bodies

Worship the Lord your God, and His blessing will be on your food and water. I will take away sickness from among you.

EXODUS 23:25

Such great promises are hidden in the Word of God concerning food! Here He promises that if we will worship Him, He will put His blessing on our food and water and take away sickness from among us.

Just think of all the sickness we have brought upon ourselves by our overeating. I developed diabetes, which has a direct connection to obesity. I know of others with high blood pressure and high cholesterol who have been told they are just inches away from heart disease. What about all those aches and pains in our knees, feet, legs, and backs from carrying around those excess pounds? How about the extra strain we put on ourselves and our babies when we start a pregnancy already many pounds overweight?

God's promise to us is that if we worship Him, He will bless our food and water and *take away sickness from among us!* So, how can we worship Him so that we become eligible for this benefit of having our sicknesses removed?

Worship springs from love, and love gives birth to obedience. I John 5:3 says, "This is love for God; to obey His commands." If we are obedient to God's commands regarding the way we should eat, then we can be sure that He will begin to remove some of these sicknesses from us. What a great promise!

Today's Tip:

Make a list of any sicknesses you have that you think are related to your overeating. Now, present them to God and ask Him to take them away as you worship Him through obedience.

Blessings we enjoy daily, and for the most of them, because they be so common, men forget to pay their praises. But let not us, because it is a sacrifice so pleasing to Him who still protects us, and gives us flowers and showers, and meat and content.
—Izaak Walton

Save Room for Dessert

He who has an ear, let him hear what the Spirit says to the churches. To him who overcomes, I will give the right to eat from the tree of life, which is in the paradise of God.

REVELATION 2:7

Listen up! God has promised us the ultimate dessert. We are to be given the right to eat of the tree of life. It's there, in the paradise of God, waiting with its luscious fruit to satisfy our souls.

What better way to top off a good meal than with a great dessert? Growing up, we seldom had dessert after dinner. There just wasn't enough money for "extras." We looked forward to family gatherings with relatives, because everyone brought their favorite dishes. They were all placed together on long tables and served buffet style, and there was always a dessert table. Our mouths would water at the sight of homemade cherry pies, chocolate chip cookies, frosted cakes and my favorite—that green, pineapple/cream cheese/walnut/jello stuff! Did your family have that green stuff, too?

Today's Tip:

Save room for God's ultimate in taste treats—the fruit of the tree of life.

We always intended to save enough room for plenty of dessert, but the main dishes looked equally as appetizing, so we usually ate so much of the main dishes that there was not room for dessert. Did that stop us? No way! We crammed in dessert until we were sick and miserable. How wise it would have been to discipline ourselves in the beginning to enjoy the final treat.

God has a real treat waiting for us! This scriptures promises that those who overcome will be given the right to eat from the tree of life. I'm going work on overcoming my urge to overeat, that way I can save room for God's great dessert!

This short, earthly life, important and significant though it may be in its setting, is no more than a prelude to a share in the timeless Life of God.
—J.B. Phillips

No More TUMS®

Heal me, O Lord, and I will be healed; save me and I will be saved, for you are the one I praise.

JEREMIAH 17:14

I have always suffered from incredible heartburn. I have eaten thousands of TUMS® and drank gallons of milk in an effort to quench the fire. No more!

I just realized today that I have not had heartburn in months. Now, I am not a doctor, so I can't give you the medical explanation for what causes heartburn. But I am convinced that heartburn results from eating too much food, too often. I used to think eating the wrong types of food caused my heartburn, but I know that is not the case for me. I still eat any type of food I want, but now I don't get heartburn. The only thing I have changed is the amount of food I eat and the frequency of my meals.

God sure is smart! He not only has a great plan for losing weight through Weigh Down™, but when we follow that plan, our bodies no longer rebel by sending burning retaliation to torture us. God does not tell us to refrain from certain activities to keep us from enjoying life. He tells us to eat in moderation because He wants us to enjoy all the wonderful flavors of food without pain like heartburn. Anytime the Father tells us "no," it is for our own good.

Just as our earthly fathers set guidelines to keep us safe from harm, our heavenly Father sets guidelines. We would do well to follow them and avoid the very thing our Father was trying to protect us from.

Today's Tip:

Make a list of changes you have noticed in your body since you began to eat properly, then thank the Father for them.

Look to your health; and if you have it, praise God and value it next to a good conscience; for health is . . . a blessing that money cannot buy; therefore value it, and be thankful for it.
—Henry Vaughan

$\mathcal{D}$isappointment

Why are you downcast, O my soul? Why so disturbed within me? Put your hope in God, for I will yet praise Him, my Savior and my God.

PSALM 42:5

Weigh Down™ has taught me to turn to God in times of disappointment, not to food. I had the opportunity to put this lesson into practice this week and, praise God, it works!

My daughter was scheduled to come from Arizona for a visit this week. It would have been the first time we had seen her in over a year and the first time since we got the news that she is going to have a baby. We were so excited! My husband had taken time off work, and I had taken a break from writing. We were set for a week of fun with our "little girl." Then we got the phone call.

Stacy was experiencing all the "joys" of pregnancy, including 24-hour morning sickness. The poor thing was too sick to even get on the airplane. We assured her that we understood and that we did not want her to travel when she was so ill, but we were broken-hearted.

In the past, a letdown like this would have sent me to live inside the refrigerator for a week. I have always sought comfort in food and have been left with a huge case of guilt and extra pounds to contend with.

Not this time! I cried, I felt down, and I even moped—but I did not run to food. Instead, I ran to God for comfort. I prayed, I read the Word, and I asked friends to pray for me. God sent the comfort I needed, and I have the joy of knowing that this time I went through a trial in a way that was pleasing to God. This time I have no guilt and no extra pounds—just peace. What a blessing!

$\mathcal{T}$oday's $\mathcal{T}$ip:

Next time disappointment sets in, dig in to God—not food!

Strengthen your patience with understanding, and look forward serenely to the joy that comes after sadness.
—Peter Damian

According to the Cleanness of My Hands

The Lord has dealt with me according to my righteousness, according to the cleanness of my hands He has rewarded me. For I have kept the ways of the Lord, I have not done evil by turning from my God.

II SAMUEL 22:21–22

I have been so blessed by God since I gave my eating habits over to Him. I have not been perfect in following the Weigh Down™ way of eating, but I have been diligent. When I fail, I repent and start over. God has rewarded me richly for this. Let me list for you the blessings He has given recently:

- I have lost 35 pounds (and counting) and have dropped several clothing sizes.
- My husband actually picked me up in his arms and carried me the other night—without groaning!
- I have been blessed with an Internet Ministry through which I have had the wonderful opportunity to encourage and challenge women around the world to live for God. We have seen the Father answer prayer for many who have sent email prayer requests.
- God prompted me to write the book you now hold in your hands and directed me to a great publisher, willing to take a chance on a first-time author.
- My walk with God is more dynamic now than it has ever been.

God has many rewards waiting for those who will keep His ways and keep their "hands clean" when it comes to sin.

Today's Tip:

List the many different ways God has blessed you since you became obedient with your eating. Take time to thank Him for blessing your "clean hands".

The more He gives, the more He desires to give.
—Placid Riccardi

Cry Me a River? I Have Cried an Ocean!

Streams of tears flow from my eyes, for your law is not obeyed.

PSALM 119:136

Tears used to frighten me. Growing up with 5 tough brothers taught me that only sissies cry—that tears are a sign of weakness. So, I learned to stuff my anger, frustration and hurt inside. Then I learned that God created tears as release for our emotions. Once I learned that crying was O.K.—I couldn't turn the tears off!

I've shed many tears over being overweight. Tears when my clothes did not fit. Tears when people stared and made rude comments. Tears when I stood on the scales. Tears when I couldn't participate in sports. Tears when boyfriends left for thinner women. Tears when I tried really hard to diet, only to fail. Tears because I would pray for God's help in losing weight, only to turn to food over and over again. All those tears because God's law was not obeyed.

Next, I shed tears of repentance. Tears at all my failures to please God. Tears of remorse over my disobedience. Tears at the realization that 20 years as a Christian, a professed child of God, had not made a difference in my adoration and commitment to food. Tears of regret for all the wasted years living in a much too large body.

I'm still shedding tears, but now they are tears of gratitude and joy! I am so thankful for The Weigh Down Workshop™ and to Gwen Shamblin for allowing God to use her to share His laws of eating. I am forever grateful to God for His patience with me until I finally surrendered my will to Him. I'm shedding tears of joy knowing that I have been forgiven, that I am obeying His laws, and that soon the results of my obedience will show on my body!

Today's Tip:

Don't be afraid to cry, remembering to thank God for the cleansing power of tears.

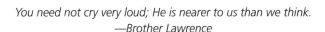

You need not cry very loud; He is nearer to us than we think.
—Brother Lawrence

Oasis

God rewards obedience. As you begin to submit your will to His Lordship, you will see Him pour out His blessings in your life. You will begin to reap the benefits of walking in obedience. It's important that you take time to acknowledge His gifts to you and to offer thanksgiving to God for His kindness.

Here are some blessings & benefits I have received.

- I no longer suffer from daily heartburn.
- I have gone from a size 20 to a size 16 dress. (And still going!)
- I have been blessed with the opportunity to write this book.

Keep a record in the space below of the blessings and benefits that you are receiving from the Lord. Take time to thank Him for them and to share with others how God rewards obedience.

Praise and Reflection

"There shall be showers of blessing . . ."
Ezekiel 34:26

Showers of Blessing

There shall be showers of blessing
Precious reviving again
Over the hills and the valleys
Sound of abundance of rain.
There shall be showers of blessing
Send them upon us, Oh Lord
Grant to us now a refreshing
Come, and now honor Thy Word

DANIEL W. WHITTLE

Reflection

Are you enjoying the blessings and benefits of obedience?

His Helping Hand

God Chose You

But you are a chosen people, a royal priesthood, a holy nation, a people belonging to God, that you may declare the praises of Him who called you out of darkness into His wonderful light.

I Peter 2:9

It's no coincidence that you hold this book in your hand at this moment. God delights in guiding His children to resources which will help them in their efforts to grow in Him. He directs the footsteps of His children.

Think back to all the circumstances which led to your salvation. Chances are there were many things and people that directed your path to the Savior. He orchestrated the whole thing. You did not choose God, He chose you. He placed in you the desire to seek out your Creator, then left you to decide if you would accept Him into your life.

God also places in us the desire to be our best for Him. It's no accident that God has led you to Weigh Down™. If you are like me, you have struggled with a weight problem for some time. You have most likely tried many methods to lose weight and have spent time asking for God's help. God has directed your footsteps to the discovery of this program, and now He leaves the decision up to you.

Will you accept His plan for eating and submit to Him in this area of your life? It's your choice. Just as He did not force salvation on you, He won't force you to eat right. But He will reward you greatly if you make the right choice!

Today's Tip:

Thank God for giving you the desire to lose weight and for leading you to His perfect plan for eating.

I do not know how the Spirit of Christ performs it, but He brings us choices through which we never-endingly change, fresh and new, into His likeness.
—Joni Eareckson Tada

HIS HELPING HAND

See, I Am Doing a New Thing

Forget the former things; do not dwell on the past. See, I am doing a new thing. Now it springs up; do you not perceive it? I am making a way in the desert and streams in the wasteland.

ISAIAH 43:18-19

Such wise words! Dwelling on the past will drag you down and hinder your forward progress. Forget it! Forget past attempts to lose weight. Forget past diet methods, diet pills and excessive exercising. They are not permanent solutions to weight control. Put them in the past, and be prepared to move on to thinness the right way.

God is doing a new thing. Weigh Down™ is a totally different concept in weight loss. It is different from the world's methods which have always failed you. Different because you are learning far more than just how to control your eating. You are learning how to submit your entire life into the hands of a loving God.

God is making a way in the desert and streams in the wasteland. You must go through the desert to reach the Promised Land, but it is God Himself who makes a way for you through the desert and provides refreshing streams of living water along the way! Each time the journey gets tough, look around. He will provide a means of reviving your strength. He does not expect you to travel this road alone, but goes with you each step of the way.

So stop dwelling on the past and move forward, keeping your eyes open for the new things God will be doing in your life.

Today's Tip:

Just this one last time, make a list of things in your past you would rather forget. Now burn the list, forget the past, and move into an exciting new future with God at your side.

I don't need someone to repair my past; I need someone to transform me—to transform is to recreate.
—Henri Boulard

God Is There in the Evening, Too

By day the Lord went ahead of them in a pillar of cloud to guide them on their way and by night in a pillar of fire to give them light, so that they could travel by day or night. Neither the pillar of cloud by day nor the pillar of fire by night left its place in front of the people.

EXODUS 13:21-22

These verses in Exodus tell us of the faithfulness of God in leading His people. Just as He offered guidance to the children of Israel, He will help us in our efforts to lose weight both day and night.

How often I start my day with a strong resolve to please God in my eating. I do well in the morning, through noon and even at dinnertime, but I have great difficulties after that. I struggle the most from dinnertime to bedtime. I want to snack while watching television and during social occasions—even when I am not hungry!

Today's Tip:

Help yourself to a second portion of God's word in the evening.

Has God left me during the evening hours? If He didn't desert the Israelites at night, then I'm sure He wouldn't desert me at night. So, I think the problem must be that in the evening I am not as diligent to follow that "pillar" He has set before me.

That pillar that guides me by day and by night is the Bible. Each morning I start the day in God's word. It strengthens me for the battle and encourages me to fight the good fight. Perhaps if I would add a second helping of His word to my evening, I would not be so apt to forget to follow the "pillar." I think I'll turn the TV off and open my Bible in the evenings for added strength!

The study of God's Word, for the purpose of discovering God's will, is the secret discipline which has formed the greatest characters.
—James W. Alexander

Jesus Is Interceding for Me

Christ Jesus, who died—more than that, who was raised to life—is at the right hand of God and is also interceding for us.

ROMANS 8:34

I can just see it now. Up there is the Almighty God of the universe seated upon His throne, and at His right hand is Jesus, His beloved Son. Jesus leans over to say something to the Father. What is it that He whispers in the ear of God?

Maybe He says something like this. "Father, look down there. It's Jan, and she is struggling with that box of chocolates. Listen to her thoughts. She is fighting to bring her stubborn will into obedience to you, Father. It's hard for her to break old habits. She isn't getting any younger, you know. Maybe we should help her out of this one."

Down on earth, I rip the box of chocolates open and discover that they have turned white and chalky with age. I bought them on sale, but I expected them to be good—not stale and inedible! I toss them in the trash can with disgust and walk away, congratulating myself for my incredible self-control. I was able to resist a whole box of chocolates!

How many times has Jesus helped me like this? How many times have I taken the credit for my strength and neglected to give thanks to Him for His help? How much more is He willing to do for me if I will just lean on Him for my strength? Thank you, Jesus, for your continual intercession for me. I certainly do need someone pulling for me—and who better than the Son of God!

Today's Tip:

Jesus Himself is interceding for you right this moment. Thank Him for presenting your cause to the Father.

Friend, you can trust the Man that died for you.
—James McConkey

Daily Burdens

Praise be to the Lord, to God our Savior, who daily bears our burdens.
PSALM 68:19

God never promised us an easy life. On the contrary, His word assures us that as Christians we may face even greater trials than those who are not Christians. Unfortunately, we often allow these burdens to drive us to eat. There is a better way!

God has promised that He will bear our daily burdens. There is a catch, however. We must be willing to give the burden over to Him; He will not take it from us.

I recall a story of a little girl with a broken doll. Tearfully, she brought it to her father, asking him to fix it for her. When he reached to take it from her, she drew back and clutched it tightly. "Sweetheart," her daddy said, "I cannot mend it properly if you will not give it to me." She slowly handed the doll to him. Anxiously, she paced as she waited for the doll to be fixed. Daddy seemed to be taking so long. Finally, the wait was just too much for her. In desperation, she snatched the doll back. It was only partially mended, but she felt comforted just to carry it once again.

Don't turn to food when you are burdened. It will not lighten your load. On the contrary, it will add to it. Instead, bring your burdens to God and leave them in His capable hands. Give Him time to work the problems out no matter how long it takes. Resist the urge to snatch the burden back once you have placed it in the Father's hands. He is more than able to fix the broken pieces of your life. Just ask him. Then, trust Him.

Today's Tip:

What burden are you clutching? Give it to the Father, and walk through life lighter.

Why should we go reeling and staggering under the burdens and cares of life when we have such prospects before us?
—D.L. Moody

HIS HELPING HAND

The Hidden Agenda

No, we speak of God's secret wisdom, a wisdom that has been hidden and that God destined for our glory before time began.

I CORINTHIANS 2:7

God is so wise! I get a kick out of the way God will let me believe He is teaching me one thing, when He is really teaching me another. I am usually in it up to my elbows before I realize that things are not as I thought in the beginning. Like this Weigh Down™ thing. I *thought* I was joining a weight loss program. Ha! Oh, I am losing weight, and fast. The quick weight loss was probably designed to keep me in Weigh Down™ long enough for God to get the real message through to me: submit your will, Jan.

I soon discovered that Weigh Down™ is more about spiritual growth than losing weight. It's about submitting my will to God, and not just in my eating, either. I prefer working on one area of self-improvement at a time, but that doesn't seem to be God's plan. Just when I start feeling all proud of myself for being submissive with eating, He exposes other areas of rebellion in my life!

God is not only reshaping my body, He is reshaping my entire being. Like the potter who shapes the vessel by pushing here and pulling there, I am being molded into a vessel He can use for His glory. Sometimes I just want to jump off the wheel. Do you think He will let me? No way!

Today's Tip:

Look for God's "hidden agenda." He wants to make you more than just thin!

Do not limit the benefit of fasting merely to abstinence from food, for a true fast means refraining from evil. Loose every unjust bond, put away your resentment against your neighbor, forgive him in his offenses. Do not let your fasting lead to wrangling and strife. You do not eat meat, but you devour your brother; you abstain from wine, but not from insults.

—Ambrose

God Uses Birdies to Do His Work

You will drink from the brook, and I have ordered the ravens to feed you there.

I KINGS 17:4

God used the birds to feed Elijah in the Old Testament. Now, thousands of years later He still finds creative ways to help us out. Even if He has to use a bird to do His work!

God wants to help us lose weight. He wants us to succeed. He will even provide help for us when we struggle to obey. In Weigh Down™, we call these our "ways of escape" from temptation. This week, my friend, Linda, related a way of escape that God provided for her.

Linda's friend invited her to join some women from her church at Women's Circle meeting. Linda was looking forward to the time of fellowship and food with much delight, because she had been really obedient that day.

They ate outdoors and the variety of food was wonderful. As she was finishing, she began to ask the Lord if it was time to stop. She thought she heard Him say yes, but questioned Him again, as she contemplated that last piece of chicken and the few chips left on her plate. Well, this time Linda did not hear the word "yes" in her conscience. Instead she heard a thud on her plate. The Lord had sent a bird to do His business on her food as a "way of escape" for her!

Yes, God will use whatever it takes to help us with those "hard" decisions. If the birds are obedient to Him, maybe we should be, too!

As in heaven your will is promptly performed, so may it be done on earth by all creatures, particularly in me and by me.
—Elizabeth of Hungary

Throw It on the Ground

Then the Lord said to him, "What is that in your hand?...Throw it on the ground."

EXODUS 4:2-3

I chuckled when I read this verse. I could just picture God catching me with food in my hand and telling me to throw on the ground? I laughed, then dismissed the thought.

That same morning I decided to dye my hair. Big mistake! The box said Warm Auburn, but my hair turned maroon! I was horrified. My niece's wedding was the next day, and I didn't want to show up with maroon hair. I raced to the drug store to get another bottle of hair dye, praying all the way that my hair would not fall out from all the chemicals.

At the checkout register, I spied my favorite butterscotch candies. I hadn't had them in a long time, so I grabbed the packet and added it to my purchases. On the way to the car, I popped one in my mouth.

Today's Tip:

As I pulled my car from the parking lot toward home, I realized that the candy tasted really old. Yuck! I took it from my mouth, rolled down the window, and threw it out. As it bounced on the road, I suddenly remembered that verse: Throw it on the ground. God is so funny! I cracked up!

Keep a sense of humor as you travel the road to thinness.

Laughter is a gift from God. Keep your eyes open and look for God to use humor as He is teaching you to eat according to His will.

By the way—my hair is now ash blonde.

Let laughter reign when it comes. It is oil for the engines that rise to challenges and work miracles.
—Donald E. Demaray

The Missing Book

All the days of the oppressed are wretched, but the cheerful heart has a continual feast.

PROVERBS 15:15

God has blessed me with a cheerful heart. That's a nice way of saying God gave me a wacky sense of humor!

I always pray before my morning Bible study for God to show me where to read. Sometimes I mentally run through the books of the Bible and stop at one if I feel prompted to read. This morning I started running through the books, and my eyes fell on my coffee cup that read "I can't take it anymore!" The words on the cup and the names of the Bible got mixed up in my head and I said out loud, "First Cantalonians (a cross between "I can't" and First Corinthians). I cracked up!

I imagined Paul writing to the Cantalonians, who were well known for saying "I can't" anytime they were faced with a challenge. Paul would be expressing his disappointment in their negative attitudes. He would remind them that "They can do all things through Christ, who gives them strength." He would chastise them for their lack of faith and their lack of willingness to try.

I know some Cantalonians, don't you? They keep mumbling, "I can't; it's too hard." If they were honest they would say, "I won't" instead of "I can't!"

I had just one problem this morning. Try as might, I couldn't find First Cantalonians in the Bible. God must have wiped those faithless people out!

Today's Tip:

Don't be a Cantalonian! Believe that you can, because Christ will give you the strength

---

Without the divine drop of oil we call humour the great world machine would soon grind to a standstill.
—Hugo Rahner

May I Take Your Plate

. . . And God is faithful; He will not let you be tempted beyond what you can bear. But when you are tempted, He will also provide a way out so that you can stand up under it.

I CORINTHIANS 10:13B

God is so good! He watches out for us wherever we go and looks for creative ways to help us with our weight loss. Here's what happened to my friend Julie when she contemplated being the "clean-up crew" for her children's left-overs.

Julie was at a McDonald's with her three children. Of course they were more interested in playing than eating. When Julie went into the playroom to help them take their shoes off, she was looking forward to finishing up the rest of their dinner. But, when she returned to their table, it had been wiped clean. Everything was gone!

Close by, an elderly McDonald's employee was clearing and wiping tables as fast as he could and truly doing a GREAT job! When he saw that Julie had come back to the table, he apologized over and over for removing their food. He even offered to replace it for her. Julie just laughed. She thought, 'If that wasn't a sign to stop eating then I don't know what is!'"

Today's Tip:

Look for the "hand of God" to remove food when you don't need it. Let your reaction be one of laughter and gratitude for His intervention.

A God wise enough to create me and the world I live in is wise enough to watch out for me.
—Philip Yancey

Take My Hand, Precious Lord

Yet I am always with you; you hold me by my right hand. You guide me with your counsel, and afterward you will take me into glory.

PSALM 73:23-24

What a blessing to know that God has us by our right hand, that He is guiding us with His counsel, and that He is taking us into glory.

I used to picture myself walking through life with the Lord. When times were hard, He would be walking behind me, pushing me onward. When I was confused, He would walk in front of me, leading the way. And when my life was going smoothly, God would stroll beside me to keep me company. I now have a new picture of Him taking me by the hand and guiding me, counseling me, then leading me to glory better than all the rest I had imagined.

Today's Tip:

Close your eyes, lift your right hand to the Father, and place it firmly in His. Now keep it there.

It reminds me of a child walking through a busy mall, holding the hand of a parent. As long as he keeps his hand tucked securely in place, he will not wander and get lost, he will not be snatched away, and he will be protected from harm. He doesn't fret about where he is going, or if he will take the right route, or get there on time. He is content to let his parent guide him as he enjoys the sights in the mall.

Let's remember that as we journey through the desert to the Promised Land. Let's keep our hand tucked firmly inside the Father's hand and walk obediently where He leads, listening to His counsel until He leads us into glory.

All created things are living in the Hand of God. The senses see only the action of the creatures; but faith sees in everything the action of God.
—Jean Pierre de Caussade

Oasis

God wants to help you lose weight. He will not leave you to fight this battle alone. When you are tempted, He will provide a way of escape from temptation. It may come in the form of a distraction, a perfectly timed accident, or a sudden strengthening of your spirit. He has used the following ways to help me control my eating.

- Perfectly timed phone calls.
- Scriptures which speak directly to my heart when I am tempted.
- Helping me to find the perfect dress for a wedding (on sale). The dress made me feel so good, I danced at the wedding instead of hanging out at the food table!

You are going to be amazed at the clever, often humorous methods God chooses to help you out of temptation. Record below the ways of escape that God provides for you on your way to thinness.

_____

_____

_____

_____

_____

_____

_____

"For as many as are led by the Spirit of God . . ."

Romans 8:14

Holy Spirit, Faithful Guide

Gently lead us by the hand
Pilgrims in a desert land
When the storms are raging sore
Hearts grow faint and hopes give o'er
Whisper softly, "Wand'rer, come!
Follow me, I'll guide thee home"

MARCUS M. WELLS

Reflection

God extends His helping hand to take you through this desert land! Reach out
and take His helping hand.

Make a Sacrifice

What Are You Holding On To?

A certain ruler asked Him, "Good teacher, what must I do to inherit eternal life?" . . . "Sell everything you have and give to the poor, and you will have treasure in heaven. Then come follow me." When he heard this, he became very sad, because he was a man of great wealth.

LUKE 18:18-23

Jesus asked this man to give up his money—not because it was evil, but because He knew it was the one thing that still held his heart. Unfortunately, the man chose to walk away and not follow Jesus. Though it saddened him, the money had a stronger hold on him than his desire to follow the Lord.

How many years did I walk in this man's shoes? I was not consumed by the love of money, but of food. Many times I went to Jesus, seeking to walk closer to Him, and many times He pointed to my love for food. I would try to give up the food but always returned to my "first love." I was more in love with food than with my Lord, and like the rich man, it saddened me, but I would not give up the food I loved.

Jesus does not ask us to give up food because it is evil. He asks us to give up our *love* of food. He sees that our love for food it is so strong that it nudges Him out of His rightful place as our "first love." He asks us to break its stronghold on our lives and submit our eating to Him. Will we do it? Or will we walk away?

Today's Tip:

He's asking you today to decide. Leave your love for food and follow Him, or go away saddened.

God does not call upon us to give up a single thing that adds to our happiness; all He wants us to give up are the things which are the blight of our lives.
—D.L. Moody

Set Up an Altar

David built an altar to the Lord there and sacrificed burn offerings and fellowship offerings. He called on the Lord, and the Lord answered him with fire from heaven on the altar of burnt offering.

I CHRONICLES 21:26

Built any altars lately? I confess, for years I carried in my body an altar to the god of Gluttony. I made frequent sacrifices to this idol, because Gluttony is a greedy god and not easily appeased.

I carried ample amounts of the sacrificial elements with me, just in case the god got restless. My car, my house, my desk drawer at work, and my purse were well stocked with goodies. As I fed this god, his altar grew. Each sacrifice piled up until the altar was breaking under the weight. Then one day, the True God asked my permission to smash the altar.

Today's Tip:

Smash all altars except the one in your heart to the True God.

I was stunned! Give up the god of my youth? Abandon the sacrificial feedings? I hesitated, until He offered a better solution—set up an altar in my heart to Him. I could make as many sacrifices to Him as I wanted daily. The sacrifices He accepted were love, obedience, my will, prayer, and praise. I agreed to the destruction of the altar to Gluttony.

I had tried to give up this gluttonous god many times before on my own, so I had my doubts. Could the True God give me strength to deny Gluttony? I decided to give it a try.

Now I carry the altar to God in my heart. I offer many sacrifices each day, and this altar has grown. But, it is not heavy; it's light. People have noticed a change in me. So, I share with them the story of my rescue from the god of Gluttony.

You can set up an altar to God in your mind by means of prayer.
And so it is fitting to pray at your trade, on a journey,
standing at a counter or sitting at your handicraft.
—John Chrysostom

Quit Hogging It All for Yourself

You have not brought any fragrant calamus (sweet cane) for me, or lavished on me the fat of your sacrifices. But you have burdened me with your sins and wearied me with your offenses.

ISAIAH 43:24

It's just human nature to want to keep the best for ourselves. God isn't asking for second-best. He is asking us to lavish on Him the sweetest, juiciest sacrifices.

When it comes to eating, it's easy to offer to God the foods we don't like. I'm hardly ever tempted to binge on celery or carrots, so offering them to God is no big deal. I'm seldom hungry in the morning, so sacrificing breakfast is easy. But, what kind of sacrifices are these?

Remember Cain and Abel? They both made sacrifices to God, but only one sacrifice was accepted. Abel brought the best he had and offered it to God while Cain withheld the best for himself. God rejected Cain's sacrifice but accepted the sacrifice of Abel.

Today's Tip:

Offer your very best to God. Don't expect Him to accept a half-hearted sacrifice.

How do you react when God asks for those last few bites of your favorite food? Is it the same reaction He would get if He asked you to sacrifice a food you don't really like? Or are you even willing to make the sacrifice at all? Let's not burden the Lord with our sin and weary Him with our offenses. How tiresome it must be for God to listen to His children profess our devotion to Him and yet go on committing the same offenses day after day. Let us instead, shower Him with sacrifices of obedience.

The sow of gluttony has piglets with these names. Too early is the name of the first, the next to fastidiously, the third too freely, the fourth is called too much, and the fifth too often.
—Ancrene Wisse

38

How Much Does a Sacrifice Cost?

Araunah said, "Why has my lord the king come to his servant?" "To buy your threshing floor" David answered, "so I can build an altar to the Lord…" Araunah said to David. "Let my lord the king take whatever pleases Him and offer it up"…But the king replied to Araunah, "No, I insist on paying you for it. I will not sacrifice to the Lord my God burnt offerings that cost me nothing."

II SAMUEL 24:21-24

David was unwilling to offer God a sacrifice that cost him nothing. The very word sacrifice indicates doing without, giving something up, self-denial. We want to lose weight, but we don't want it to hurt. We are unwilling to deny ourselves the huge amounts of food we are used to consuming. We don't want to have to give up anything! Now, what kind of sacrifice is that?

When I choose to do God's will instead of my own, I am sacrificing my will. But not all sacrifices are acceptable to God. Much depends on the attitude of my heart as I make the sacrifice. It is this attitude which makes a sacrifice acceptable or unacceptable in God's eyes. A willing, humble sacrifice pleases the Father, but a sacrifice made grudgingly with resentment is an offense to God. I will not offend my Lord with a sacrifice which costs me nothing or with an attitude which insults Him.

God does not *require* sacrifices, but I am sure He is *pleased* when we offer our desire to overeat to Him as a sacrifice. When my head is telling me to eat something my stomach says I don't need, I can make this a sacrifice unto the Lord. I can offer it up with praise and thanksgiving. This sacrifice costs me my will, but it is the attitude with which I make the sacrifice that matters to God!

Today's Tip:

Do not offer to God that which costs you nothing. Consider making your trash can an altar on which to sacrifice excess food. And do it with a grateful heart.

Great holiness demands great sacrifice.
—Barbara Fiand

Doing Without—On Purpose

Then Jesus said to His disciples, "If anyone would come after me, he must deny himself and take up his cross and follow me."

MATTHEW 16:24

Jesus asks us to carry our cross. It's not a cross made of splintered wood, such as the one He carried to Calvary; it is the cross of self-denial. It's not heavy, but it sure is awkward!

It doesn't feel right to say "no" to our natural, human impulses. We are creatures who love pleasure and avoid pain at all costs. We want to feel good and do all the things that bring us pleasure. You know the old motto: If it feels good—do it!

Yet, God tells us to control our desires. He doesn't ask us to *abstain* from all pleasure, rather to enjoy the pleasures of this world within the boundaries of His guidelines. Therein lies the problem; we do not want boundaries. We want to be free to indulge in anything, anytime, in any amount that seems right to us.

Jesus carried His cross. It was the cross of obedience to the Father's will. He did not wait to pick up the cross on the day of His crucifixion, nor did He cease to carry it after His resurrection. He carried that cross all the days He walked on this earth. He remained obedient through life, death, and life after death. He is our example.

Let us carry our cross of self-denial and obedience, no matter how awkward, through life, through death, and straight into eternity.

The cross that Jesus tells us to carry is the one that we willingly take up ourselves—the cross of self-denial in order that we might live for the glory of the Father.
—Colin Urquhart

MAKE A SACRIFICE

What Percentage Do You Give?

Jesus replied: "Love the Lord your God with all your heart and with all your soul and with all your mind."

MATTHEW 22:37

God wants all of us. He wants our heart, our soul, and our mind. He wants everything we are, not just a part. He wants all of our love and devotion. He wants all of our will.

Have you ever seen a pie chart? (Why is everything in this world related to food?) Well, what if you drew a pie chart to determine how to divide up what you give to God? How much of your heart, soul, and mind do you give to Him, and how much is given to the things of this world? How much of your love and devotion are directed toward God and how much toward others or ourselves? And what about the *biggie*—what about our will? What size is the slice of that pie that reflects the percentage of your will that you surrender to God? 10%? 25%? 50%? 75%? 99.9%?

He wants it all! 100%! He is not greedy. He doesn't want it all just so He will have more and you will be empty. He wants you to empty yourself so that He can fill you up with His heart and soul and mind. He wants to give you all His love and devotion, and He wants to fill you with His will.

How much empty space have you created in your heart to make room for God to pour His blessings in?

Today's Tip:

Draw a pie chart reflecting the portion of your time, thoughts, love, and will that you give to God. Reflect on how you can give more so that you can receive more from Him.

Love Him totally who gave Himself totally for your love.
—Clare of Assisi

An Undivided Heart

"Teach me your way, O Lord, and I will walk in your truth; give me an undivided heart, that I may fear your name."

PSALM 86:11

It's hard to have a divided heart. I grew up in Ohio but lived 11 years in Arizona. I have dear friends and family in both states and often feel pulled between the two.

Phoenix, Arizona is beautiful and rugged. Majestic mountains rise like fortress walls around the city, where there is always plenty to do and life moves at an exhilarating speed. My daughter and son-in-law live in Phoenix, as do my dear friends, Joan and Allene. I often long to see them and feel the warmth of the Arizona sunshine on my face, especially on a cold Ohio morning!

Ohio is my home state. I love the change of the seasons. Just when you get tired of one, a new one comes along to cheer you up. Life in Ohio is slower, friendlier, and a lot more "country." Folks still chat with their neighbors over the backyard fence. They still gather on the front porch in the evenings and wave as you go by, even if they don't know you. After 11 years in Arizona, I longed to move "back home" but then was confused—just where was home?

When our hearts are pulled in two directions, we can never fully commit to either one. It's like that with those of us who have given food too big of a chunk of our heart. God wants our whole heart, but years of devotion to food keep calling us back. We must make up our minds to be fully devoted to God, for He will not share our heart with another love. He will not allow a divided heart.

Today's Tip:

Draw a heart and write God's name inside. Put it on your refrigerator to remind you that you only have one love.

If your heart is not clear and undivided—'single', as Jesus put it—then it will be weak.
—Eberhard Arnold

MAKE A SACRIFICE

Oasis

Sometimes it takes sacrificial giving to make a spiritual break-through. If you find yourself really struggling to give up your will, you might want to try a 48-hour fast. Now, don't get scared! I'm not talking about giving up all food for 48 hours (unless God directs you to do so). But, I have found that some of us are addicted to certain things. They are controlling us instead of us controlling them.

It might be television, talking on the phone, surfing the 'Net, soda pop, cigarettes, coffee. (No, wait! Not coffee! Yikes!) Whatever it is, if you think it is controlling you, it could be a stronghold that God wants you to break. Pray about it and ask God if there is anything that He would like you to give up for 48 hours (or whatever amount of time He directs). You will be surprised at the amount of control you will feel after a 48-hour fast.

List below anything that you think might be a stronghold that God wants you to break. Then pray about making it a sacrifice to God.

Present your bodies a living sacrifice, holy, acceptable to God . . .

Romans 12:1

Is Your All on the Altar?

You have longed for sweet peace
And for faith to increase
And have earnestly, fervently prayed
But you cannot have rest
Or be perfectly blest
Until all on the altar is laid
O we never can know
What the Lord will bestow
Of the blessings for which we have prayed
Till our body and soul
He doth fully control
And our all on the altar is laid

ELISHA A. HOFFMAN

Reflection

Is there any part of your life that has not been laid on the altar?

Simple Obedience

Ignorance Isn't Bliss

As obedient children, do not conform to the evil desires you had when you lived in ignorance.

I PETER 1:14

We once lived in ignorance. We battled our addiction to food with man-made diet plans. We went on every crazy diet that came out. If a celebrity lost 10 pounds eating kumquats, we rushed right out and bought a bushel of kumquats. If the experts said we could lose 15 pounds overnight by encasing our bodies in plastic wrap, we mummified ourselves. What ignorance!

We fought to get our heavy bodies into shape with exercise regimens—walking, running, and yoga. We poured our money into health spas, workout videos and exercise equipment, which sat gathering dust in the corner after the first month. All the while, we were giving in to our evil desires to eat, eat, eat. Ignorance!

Today's Tip:

Shed any remaining ignorance and be obedient to God's plan for eating.

Living in ignorance and conforming to desires is normal for someone who is not a child of God, but if you're His, the time has come to be obedient children. How many times could your child get away with disobedience if you told him no cookies before dinner and yet you continually caught him with his hand in the cookie jar? The innocent look on that little face might melt your heart the first few times, but his sincere "I forgot," or "it's just too hard" would loose its sincerity after repeated offenses. Discipline would soon be in order.

We want obedient children and so does God! We are no longer ignorant about how God wants us to care for our bodies by eating in moderation. He has shown us how He wants us to eat. Now we must be obedient children and do what He has asked us to do. Let's discipline ourselves, so God doesn't have to do it for us!

It is worse still to be ignorant of your ignorance.
—Jerome

God Tests Our Obedience

Then the Lord said to Moses, "I will rain down bread from heaven for you. The people are to go out each day and gather enough for that day. In this way I will test them and see whether they will follow my instructions."

EXODUS 16:4

In this passage, we see that God gave food in abundance. He rained down bread from heaven. However, He instructed the people to take only what they needed for that day. He was testing their obedience.

Why did God need to test them to see if they would follow His instructions? I'm sure God knew beforehand what would happen. He knows the hearts of His children. He wants to reveal to us what's hidden in our hearts. The problem is that *we* don't know where our hearts stand until we are tested. This test revealed the greed and lack of faith in the hearts of the people.

We learn two lessons from this scripture. First, God wants us to depend on Him daily for our needs. He wants us to trust Him to provide for us, not to struggle to provide for ourselves. Does that mean we can be lazy and lay back waiting for God to drop what we need into our laps? No. The Israelite children did have to go out and gather what He had provided. God does not appreciate laziness any more than self-indulgence.

Second, God sent down more manna than the people actually needed. He still provides food in abundance, and He still uses it to test the obedience of His children. What do you do when faced with an abundance of food? Are you faithful to follow His instructions for eating, or do you fail the test?

Today's Tip:

The next time you are faced with an abundance of food, consider it an opportunity to prove your obedience to your God.

For God to explain a trial would be to destroy its object, which is that of calling forth simple faith and implicit obedience.
—Alfred Edersheim

No Rest for the Disobedient

And to whom did God swear that they would never enter His rest if not to those who disobeyed?

HEBREWS 3:18

There is no rest for the disobedient! Now, I have to admit that I like my rest. I would rather be sitting on my lawn swing, reading a good book than out weeding in my garden. I would rather be floating on an air mattress in the pool than swimming laps. I would rather walk than jog. You get the picture? So, this warning of never entering into God's rest if we disobey came as quite an eye-opener for me.

The children of Israel wandered in the desert for 40 years! Not because God did not know the way to the Promised Land but because of their disobedience. They followed the pillar of fire by day and a cloud by night. Any time the fire or cloud moved, the whole camp had to pack up and start walking. It doesn't sound like they got much rest on the journey!

Today's Tip:

Want to rest in the promises of God? Stay obedient!

It wasn't bad enough that they had to wander through sand and cactus most of their lives, but just as they approached the Promised Land, they were informed that they would not be permitted to enter it. Only their children, who had not been disobedient, would be able to go in, take the land, and rest in its riches. What a bummer!

I want to enter the Promised Land. My Promised Land is to be free from overeating, to no longer feel controlled by food, and to rest in the knowledge that I am pleasing God. The only thing that can keep me from reaching this place of rest is my own disobedience. God has promised rest for the obedient, but He has also promised there would be no rest for those who disobey. I choose the former!

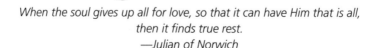

When the soul gives up all for love, so that it can have Him that is all, then it finds true rest.
—Julian of Norwich

SIMPLE OBEDIENCE

Oh, To Be Steadfast

You have laid down precepts that are to be fully obeyed. Oh, that my ways were steadfast in obeying your decrees!

PSALM 119 4–5

It is my heart's desire to be steadfast in obeying God. Alas, I am not. I have all the best intentions of obeying, then find myself at the foot of the cross, confessing my failure to follow the precepts He has laid before me. It's a daily battle to be steadfast in obeying God.

God has laid down precepts that are to be *fully* obeyed. Oh, how I wish I were fully obedient and would do the things that please Him! I want to keep myself from giving in to my fleshly desires. I try hard, but I keep failing. Sometimes I wonder how the Lord puts up with me at all! But then I remember Jesus.

I remember that Jesus was the only perfect man to walk this earth. Jesus was the only one who remained steadfast in fully obeying God's laws. Because of this, Jesus was the only one qualified to make the final sacrifice for our sins. It was our sin that required this sacrifice. And it was His perfection which purchased my forgiveness.

Today's Tip:

Strive for full obedience, but when you fall short, fall at the foot of the cross.

I am not perfect, and I cannot expect perfection in obeying God. But, I can strive for it. I can and will keep trying every day to do the things that I know God wants me to do. I know there will be times when I fail, but now I know how to handle that failure.

When my ways fall short of full obedience, Lord, I come to you in true repentance. I am eternally grateful that there was one who was steadfast in obeying your decrees—the one who provided a way back to you when I stumble in disobedience. Thank you for giving your Son.

God had one Son without sin, but He never had a Son without trial.
—Charles Spurgeon

Slave or Servant?

For he who was a slave when he was called by the Lord is the Lord's freed-man; similarly, he who was a free man when he was called is Christ's slave.

I CORINTHIANS 7:22

My brother made a comment today that made me think. (A difficult task.) He said, "Until you are willing to be a servant, you will always be a slave to something." Isn't that an amazing statement? How did he get so smart?

He was right. Until I was willing to set aside my will and choose to serve God, I was a slave to sin. Once I chose to serve, the chains of slavery were broken, or at least most of them were. God would have loved to free me from *all* the chains in my life, but I was not willing to serve God in *all* areas. For years, I continued to be a slave to food, because I refused to give up my will in this area.

Today's Tip:

It's your choice—slavery or servanthood. Which will you choose?

Food is a hard master. Its hold on you is strong. It entices you to over-indulge yourself with its rich tastes and abundance. However, what starts out as pleasure soon becomes agony. Your body swells, and the chains tighten. Freedom seems impossible, but it is within your reach!

God offers you the opportunity to serve Him. He invites you to leave other masters behind and to become His servant. As a loving master, He will care for you and love you because once you become His servant, He considers you His child.

Grasp the opportunity to give yourself to God. Be willing to be obedient to Him where food is concerned, and the chains of slavery will drop at your feet. You will feel a delicious freedom, and soon your body will return to its normal size.

Be both a servant, and free: a servant in that you are subject to God, but free in that you are not enslaved to anything.
—John of Apamea

What's the Bottom Line?

Why do you call me, "Lord, Lord," and do not do what I say?

LUKE 6:46

The bottom line here is obedience. I can talk all I want about God's Word and God's will, but if I don't put it into practice, He is not really my Lord.

For God to be Lord of your life, He must have an affect on how you live every part of your life. You must consider His will when deciding what kind of entertainment you permit in your life, what kind of clothing you wear, how you conduct yourself in relationships, and how you conduct business. Yes, you should even consider God's will in the very food you eat! Just knowing His will is not good enough—we must be willing to do it!

In eighth grade, I had a wonderful math teacher, Mrs. Marsh. She was kind and gentle and explained math so well, that for the first time I fully understood mathematics. The problem was that she was so kind, she never insisted that I turn in my homework. I was lazy and failed the first grading period. I remember standing in shame as Mrs. Marsh explained that although she knew I understood the principles of solving math problems, she could not grade me on what I knew, only what I did. Head knowledge is only good if applied.

Today's Tip:

Get God's word out of your head and into your heart, then it will effect your life.

God will not judge you on what you know, but on what you do. If knowing His will doesn't make any changes in your actions, perhaps you need to consider whether He really is *Lord* of your life.

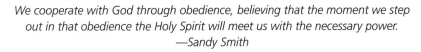

We cooperate with God through obedience, believing that the moment we step out in that obedience the Holy Spirit will meet us with the necessary power.
—Sandy Smith

Praying for Obedience

Now reform your ways and your actions and obey the Lord your God.
JEREMIAH 26:13A

Recently, I was looking back over my Weigh Down™ workbook from the first session. I started reading the prayer requests each one in the group had given, thinking it would be interesting to see how many of our prayers had been answered since then. One prayer request was repeated by many in the group (including me) week after week. "Please pray that I will be obedient to God in my eating this week."

Can we pray to be obedient? If we pray for group members to be obedient, and they are not, does that mean God did not answer our prayers? Can we really ask God to *make* us obey Him? Do we really think He will do that?

Remember, God gave us a free will. He did not create a race of robots, but humans—free to make our own choices. I believe obedience is a choice. God has already given us everything we need to be able to obey Him. He will not force obedience. He does, however, reward obedience, just as He punishes disobedience.

"See, I am setting before you today a blessing and a curse—the blessing if you obey the commands of the Lord your God . . . the curse if you disobey the commands of the Lord your God." Deuteronomy 11:26–28

I don't think I will be asking my Weigh Down™ group to pray again that I will be obedient. I will not ask God to do for me what He expects me to do for myself.

A demanding spirit, with self-will as its rudder, blocks prayer . . .
—Catherine Marshall

You Were Bought with a Price

Do you not know that your body is a temple of the Holy Spirit, who is in you, whom you received from God? You are not your own, you were bought with a price. Therefore honor God with your body.

I Corinthians 6:19–20

Oh, the price that was paid to rescue the rebellious will of man! We had it all: a beautiful garden to live in, sunshine to bless our days, soft moonlight and twinkling stars to grace our nights, great seas of water with cooling breezes and sandy beaches, trees and plants that produced fruits and seeds to eat, and every creature which walked on the earth for our amusement. Man had woman and woman had man for blessed companionship. Best of all, God walked with us in the cool of the evening in sweet fellowship. What more could we want?

There was only one thing that God asked of man. Many will think of the forbidden fruit, but the one thing God asked was obedience. He didn't force obedience, He asked. He didn't build a barrier around that forbidden tree, but gave man the freedom to choose obedience or disobedience. We made the wrong choice. I cannot blame Eve, for I too have been tempted by the enemy to eat more than what God intended for me to eat.

In the Bible, committing a sin required that a sacrifice be made. It was Adam and Eve's sin, my sin, the sin of each of us which required the sacrifice. Then God in His infinite love provided the sacrifice: His perfect Son. Oh, what a great price to ransom my willful, disobedient spirit!

In light of that great sacrifice, can we refuse to maintain our body (His temple) in a clean and honorable state?

Today's Tip:

What things are cluttering up your temple? Let's sweep them clean and determine to keep our temples honorable through obedience.

It costs God nothing, so far as we know, to create nice things; but to convert rebellious wills cost Him crucifixion.
—C.S. Lewis

I'm Praying for You

I keep asking that the God of our Lord Jesus Christ, the glorious Father, may give you the Spirit of wisdom and revelation, so that you may know Him better. I pray also, that the eyes of your heart may be enlightened in order that you may know the hope to which He has called you, the riches of His glorious inheritance in the saints, and His incomparably great power for us who believe.

EPHESIANS 1:17–19

I am so excited about what God is teaching me through Weigh Down™, that I am praying that everyone who fights this continual battle with overeating will find what I have found. Weigh Down™ gave me the tools to learn obedience to God, but it was God that gave me the wisdom to know these same tools can be applied to every area of struggle in my life.

My husband is a "tool man." Sears reserves a special parking place for Lee with his name on it. His workshop is well stocked with every imaginable tool, but there is always just one more tool he needs to do the job right. It would be great if there was just one "super-tool" to do it all. A combination, screwdriver-wrench-drill-saw-hammer type thing. What a handy tool that would be!

Weigh Down™ has provided me with just such a tool. This tool has helped me fight fear and anger. It has taught me to control my tongue and keep it from gossip and complaining. It has strengthened my walk with God, and loosened the grip of sin in my life. It may have started with food, but now it fills my life, this wonderful super-tool called obedience!

I pray that God will reveal to you the power of this super-tool to repair the problems in your life. I guess that bumps Lee out of first place as the "Tool Man!"

Today's Tip:

See just how many sins you can fix in your life with the super-tool of obedience.

Have thy tools ready; God will find thee work.
—Charles Kingsley

SIMPLE OBEDIENCE

Oasis

God wants obedience—plain and simple. Unfortunately, we are by nature disobedient children. It's easy to get discouraged by our acts of disobedience. It's easy to dwell on our failures and overlook our successes. We need to confess and repent when we disobey God, but then we must put it behind us. We must focus on the times we have been obedient so that we can be encouraged that we are on the right track.

Most of the time our obedience outweighs our disobedience (or it should). Please record below times when you were tempted to disobey God, but instead chose the right path. Review this list when you are tempted again to disobey, or if you find that you have made a wrong choice and gave into temptation. This will reassure you and encourage you to chose obedience in the future.

Praise and Reflection

Now the Lord of peace Himself give you peace . . .

II Thessalonians 3:16

Wonderful Peace

Far away in the depths of my spirit tonight
Rolls a melody sweeter than psalm
In celestial like strains it unceasingly falls
O'er my soul like an infinite calm
Peace! Peace! Wonderful peace
Coming down from the Father above
Sweep over my spirit forever I pray
In fathomless billows of love

W.D. CORNELL

Reflection

Simple obedience to God will bring you untold peace.

Attitude Adjustments

He's Got High Hopes

Therefore, since we have such a hope, we are very bold.

II Corinthians 3:12

Come on, now, sing with me—"Just what makes that little old ant think he can move a rubber tree plant? Everyone knows an ant can't move a rubber tree plant, but he's got high hopes, he's got high hopes...."

I had just about given up hope. Endless diets and failures had beaten me down. I really didn't believe that I could ever be thin again—then I heard about God's way of eating. After reading *The Weigh Down Diet*, there was a glimmer of hope, just a spark. I felt much like that tiny little ant, facing a giant that must be moved. I had mounds of fat to remove, but if that ant could tackle that rubber tree plant, I can take off this weight, because I have high hopes, too.

You see, my hope is in the Lord. He is the one who lifts my hopes on high. He is the one who encourages me to try and to persevere. Suppose that ant had stepped up to that huge plant, given it a mighty push and it only budged a smidge. What if he had given up then? He sure wouldn't have had his own hit song!

Today's Tip:

Get just as determined as that little old ant and see your mountain move!

But he didn't give up. He rolled up the sleeves of his little ant shirt and pushed and shoved with all his little ant might, until he finally got that rubber tree plant just where he wanted it, one smidge at a time. That's what I am going to do. I'm going to roll up my sleeves and keep pushing and shoving my way to my normal weight. I'm going to do it, even if I have to do it one ounce at a time!

Who knows, maybe someone will write a song about me!

Patience and diligence, like faith, remove mountains.
—William Penn

You Are What You Think You Are

For as he thinketh in his heart, so is he . . .

PROVERBS 23:7 (KJV)

You are what you think you are, or at least you are on your way to becoming it.

I've known beautiful, trim women, who thought of themselves as ugly or fat. They stopped taking care of themselves, dressed sloppily and were depressed. I've also known plain, overweight women, who thought they were beautiful. They were perfectly groomed, carried themselves with distinction and radiated confidence. Each lived out what they believed.

Being 75 pounds overweight made me feel ugly. I hated myself. One day a preacher taught on loving your neighbor as you loved yourself. I knew I had a problem, so I asked God to teach me to love myself, so that I could truly love others. He impressed me to begin to act as if I loved myself, and it would happen.

Today's Tip:

Write down what you would like to become in God, then begin to act as if you were already that person, or as my friend Cathy would say, "fake it 'til you make it!"

I am going to reveal my secret trick, but please don't tell anyone I did this. Every time I passed a mirror, I would smile, give myself a wink, and say, "Lookin' good, babe!" I felt really goofy, but it made me laugh, and soon, I began to feel better about myself. Before I knew it, that feeling of despair left me. I did love myself! God had answered my prayer.

I am applying this secret technique to being thin. I am eating like a thin person. I act as if I am thin. I practice saying, "Oh, my, I'm getting full already!" or "Oh, I couldn't possibly eat that much!" Amazingly, Ii's working! I feel thin, and what I'm doing is having an effect on how much I eat and how I carry myself. I am becoming what I believe I am.

All mortals tend to turn into the thing they are pretending to be.
—C.S. Lewis

Rah-rah Sis-boom-ba!

Therefore encourage one another and build each other up, just as in fact you are doing.

I THESSALONIANS 5:11

I was never exactly "cheerleader material" in high school. Too many pounds and not enough perk, I guess. I did try out once in Jr. High. I'm not sure what was more humiliating, not making the squad or how I must have looked in those short skirts.

Anyway, I have become a self-appointed cheerleader. When my husband has a hard day at work and comes home worn out, I make it a point to tell him that I am on his team, that I am proud of him and that I appreciate all his hard work. I remind him that God will reward him for his dedication to provide for his family. I'm his number one fan!

I have always done the same for my daughter. From her teen years to her recent position as a young wife, I have always cheered her on to be all that she can be for Christ. Each time I do, I see her rise to the challenge and conquer the hurdles of life.

Recently, it occurred to me that I need to be my own cheerleader. I need to give myself a few pats on the back, a few "atta girls" and "way to goes". Speaking positively to yourself is essential to overcoming all the negatives that assault you from the outside and those that float through your head on the inside. Give yourself a pep-talk, cheer yourself on, and listen closely. I'll bet you will hear the voice of God sending up a few cheers of his own!

Today's Tip:

This is silly, but do it anyway! Make up a short cheer about yourself, and use it any time you need a boost!

Keep company with the more cheerful sort of the Godly; there is no mirth like the mirth of believers.
—Richard Baxter

Caution ~~Men~~ God at Work

For it is God who works in you to will and to act according to His good purpose. Do everything without complaining or arguing.

PHILIPPIANS 2:13–14

God is at work in us to conform us to His will and to bring about good in our lives, but this "character construction" can be frustrating.

Here in Ohio, summer means road construction. Our snowy winters play havoc with our streets, and leave crater-sized potholes come spring. Each summer, the state rolls out ugly orange construction barrels and narrows our streets down to one lane while they make repairs. We understand that this is necessary to make our roads better, but it can be very irritating. Tempers flair as traffic backs up, and threatens to make us late for work. The smell of hot tar and exhaust fumes mix to a nauseating stench.

Today's Tip:

Usually, I sit behind the wheel of my car and complain loudly. My husband, on the other hand, slips his favorite praise tape into the stereo and sings happily as he waits. He drives me crazy!

Experienced a bit of "road rage" lately? Better slip into some praise!

I need to adopt his attitude while God is doing His construction on me. If I would just relax and praise the Lord as I wait for God to take this excess weight off me I would be much happier. I would eventually get to my destination and would please God during the journey. Instead, I tend to focus on the inconveniences and frustrations along the way.

I guess I had better take a cue from my hubby and take my eyes off the construction process and start praising God for the wonderful work He is doing to make my life better.

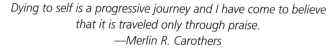

Dying to self is a progressive journey and I have come to believe that it is traveled only through praise.
—Merlin R. Carothers

The Thrill of Victory— The Agony of De "feet"

Pride goes before destruction, a haughty spirit before a fall.

PROVERBS 16:18

Humility is so humbling! Just when I was feeling so proud of myself, I suddenly found myself brought back down to earth—literally!

This week we had our church picnic at a local park. I was determined not to overeat, which is my usual custom at picnics. There were tables full of delicious foods. Burgers sizzled on the grill; baked beans, salads and homemade rolls flirted with me; cakes, pies and brownies sweetly called my name. But I was determined!

I chose carefully from among the tempting delicacies, taking only tiny portions of the best of the best. I savored every morsel and stopped eating the minute I felt that nudge from the Lord. I was flying high in my victory. I had survived the church picnic with my obedience in tact! I was proud!

I decided to play with my cousin's tiny poodle while the others finished their meal. This was just my way of drawing attention to the fact that I was no longer eating. Then it happened. I started to run as little "Chuckie" chased me, when I stumbled over a tree root. I somersaulted across the lawn like a pumpkin, landing flat on my back with my arms outstretched. I just missed landing on Chuckie, who was so excited by the chase, that he stood over my arm and relieved himself!

I had succeeded in drawing the attention of my church family, and now they howled at my embarrassing predicament. Now that's humbling!

Today's Tip:

Remember to stay humble while losing weight. It doesn't pay to show off!

We are told by all spiritual writers that one important point to bear in mind, as we seek to attain humility, is not to be surprised by our own faults and failures.
—François Fénelon

Do I Sound Like That?

In the desert the whole community grumbled against Moses and Aaron. The Israelites said to them, "If only we had died by the Lord's hand in Egypt! There we sat around pots of meat and ate all the food we wanted, but you have brought us out into this desert to starve this entire assembly to death!"

EXODUS 16:2–3

Whine! Whine! Whine! Those Israelites acted like God had brought them to the desert just to torture them. Didn't they remember that His whole purpose was to take them out of slavery to Egypt and lead them to the Promised Land? There just happened to be a desert between Egypt and their destination. Did they think God would fly them over the desert? They should have kept their minds focused on where they were headed, not the hardships of the journey.

Today's Tip:

Listen closely for any unspoken grumbling in your heart. God hears it!

You won't hear me whining like those Israelites. *You* won't, but I am afraid God does. I don't whine audibly, but my spirit is whining just the same. God hears it. God knows. He sees it in my attitude toward those around me. How did I treat my co-worker who innocently offered me a candy bar? What was that look I gave my husband when he took a second helping of lasagna? Why do I snap when I say, "No thank you, I'm not hungry"? What about the time I wondered if God was trying to starve me to death while waiting for the growl?

I wonder sometimes if He doesn't roll His eyes at me and say, "Oh, why don't you GROW UP!" I guess I am a bit like those Israelites, expecting God to take me from Egypt to the Promised Land while bypassing the desert. I guess it's my turn to stop whining!

Nothing ousts the sense of God's presence so thoroughly as the soul's dialogues with itself—when these are grumblings, grievances, etc.
—Friedrich von Hügel

You Can't Make Me

See, I am sending an angel ahead of you to guard you along the way and to bring you to the place I have prepared. Pay attention to him and listen to what He says. Do not rebel against him. . .

EXODUS 23:20–21A

Recently during my early morning prayers, I found myself confessing to God that once again I had eaten when I was not hungry. I asked Him to show me what my problem was in some tangible way.

That evening my husband and I hopped in the car to go to the store. He said, "You better stop and get some gas." (He has this annoying habit of always checking my gas gauge, because he has had to "rescue" me many times.) My response was, "Stop telling me what to do. I don't have to stop if I don't want to. You can't make me!" I was just kidding of course; I fully intended to stop. (I hate walking with that ugly red gas can in my hand!) Yet, I forgot to stop.

The next morning when I jumped in the car, I took one look at that gas gauge and groaned. "What a foolish woman I am, God. You even had Lee remind me to get gas, and I didn't do it." What was it I said? "Stop telling me what to do. I don't have to stop if I don't want to. You can't make me!" Then God said, "That's just what you say to me about your eating." Oh, I don't actually say that out loud to God, but my actions scream it loud and clear.

I prayed all the way to the gas station! I prayed that my attitude toward God would change and that I would not have to call my husband and tell him I had run out of gas!

Today's Tip:

Listen for those warning signs that God sends you. Be swift to obey.

If we do not listen we do not come to truth.
If we do not pray we do not even get as far as listening.
—Hubert van Zeller

ATTITUDE ADJUSTMENTS

Greedy Gus

Then he said, "This is what I'll do. I will tear down my barns and build bigger ones, and there I will store all my grain and my goods." And I'll say to myself, "You have plenty of good things laid up for many years. Take life easy; eat, drink and be merry." But God said to him, "You fool!"

LUKE 12:19 20

Greedy Gus—that's what this man was. He just wanted to hoard his possessions and kick back to take life easy. There's no mention of helping others, no thanks to God for what he has—just greed. Things have not changed much in 2000 years, have they?

Who says that we are supposed to get to a point in our lives where we kick back, eat, drink, and be merry? At what age does God say we can retire from doing His work? And since God is the source for all we have, how can we justify hoarding everything for ourselves?

Today's Tip:

Lest I sound too pious, let me tell you that this was my attitude toward food. Get a bigger pantry; you can never have too many canned goods. Stock the freezer; there's a sale on beef! I'd spend a fortune at the grocery store, then go out to eat most of the week. Every event was an excuse to eat, drink, and be merry. The more I ate, the merrier I thought I would be, but that's not what happened. The more I hoarded and consumed food, the more miserable I became!

When you find yourself the recipient of God's abundance, look around. There's probably someone nearby that God would like you to share it with.

God's provisions are not to be hoarded. They're to be accepted with thanksgiving and shared freely. This idea of sharing with others may not be the philosophy we hear broadcast today, but it is the core of the Christian faith.

Hunger and thirst are healthy drives unless you eat and drink solely for your own pleasure and in excess of what is reasonable. We must eat to live, and not live to eat.
—Michel Quoist

Selfish Gain

Turn my heart toward your statutes and not toward selfish gain.

PSALM 119:36

Overweight people are the most generous and the most selfish people on earth. (Speaking only from personal experience here.) I would have given my husband the shirt off my back, but I had to fight the urge to break his fingers for snatching some of my cashews! And heaven help the unfortunate person who discovered and delved into my secret stash of chocolate raisins! I even had a hard time sharing a large tub of popcorn with my husband during a movie!

I used to have a monster in my head that wanted to lash out when my child asked, "Mommy, can I have a bite?" of the huge bowl of ice cream in my lap. It's awful to admit that I used to be like this. It's embarrassing, but I would hazard a guess that I am not the only one reading this journal who has ever had this problem. What did this selfish attitude lead to? Why, of course, right down the road to "selfish gain." And boy did I gain!

I am grateful for the Weigh Down™ program, which has turned my heart toward the Lord's statutes and away from selfish gains. It has led me into a deeper study of God's Word. His truths burn in my heart now, and the selfishness is pushed out. I have no problem sharing my food with others now. Why, just the other day, I cut my slice of carrot cake in three portions to share with my niece and my husband. You would have had to hog-tie me years ago to get even a bite! Come on, I can't be the only one who ever acted like this!

Today's Tip:

If sharing food is difficult for you, beware—selfish gains are on their way!

Our gifts are not to be measured by the amount we contribute,
but by the surplus kept in our own hand.
—Charles Spurgeon

Just between You and Me

When you fast, do not look somber as the hypocrites do, for they disfigure their faces to show men they are fasting. I tell you the truth, they have received their reward in full. But when you fast, put oil on your head and wash your face, so that it will not be obvious to men that you are fasting, but only to your Father, who is unseen; and your Father, who sees what is done in secret, will reward you.

MATTHEW 6:16–18

Just between us, don't you hate being with someone who is dieting? Hunger and self-denial turns dieters into real bears. I can say this, because I have been guilty of such behavior. In the old days, my family would run for cover when I announced I was going on a diet.

Each day of the diet my mood progressively darkened. Hunger and self-denial were concepts foreign to my nature. My irritation grew, and I wanted everyone to share in my suffering. My family was denied the right to bring any "good" foods into the house. If I smelled chocolate on someone's breath, it would be their last breath. Finally, I would toss the diet aside for a hot fudge sundae, and the world would heave a sigh of relief.

Today's Tip:

Keep your attitude in check as you lose weight, and God will reward you greatly.

Those days are gone. Since I have learned to eat God's way, very few people would know I am trying to lose weight by the way I act or eat. I eat anything I want as long as I'm hungry, so I do not feel deprived. As I submit my will to God in obedience, He rewards me with sweet joy. My mood is great, and my reward comes from God in the form of weight loss.

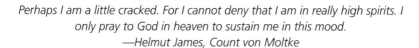

Perhaps I am a little cracked. For I cannot deny that I am in really high spirits. I only pray to God in heaven to sustain me in this mood.
—Helmut James, Count von Moltke

I Hated My Hair

But our citizenship is in heaven. And we eagerly await a Savior from there, the Lord Jesus Christ, who, by the power that enables Him to bring everything under His control, will transform our lowly bodies so that they will be like His glorious body.

PHILIPPIANS 3:20–21

What part of your body do you hate? Seems like everyone hates something about their body. For me it was my hair. I always dreamed of having long, luxurious Farrah Fawcett-like hair. What I got, was thin, fine Don Knotts type hair! I wouldn't mind it so much if I were a guy. My husband is almost bald, and it looks great on him. On me it looks funny—not funny ha-ha—funny weird. But, I have finally learned to live with my locks (or lack of them). I couldn't change them, so I accepted them.

Today's Tip:

If you can't change it, accept it. If you can change it, do it!

I almost came to believe that about my weight. It seemed that years of dieting had not made my body any thinner, so I had resigned myself to the fact that I must accept my obesity along with my thin hair. Thank God, that's not true! I *can* change my weight. I just had to learn that dieting would not do it. I had to allow God to bring me under His control. This meant submitting my will to Him, which took courage on my part. At first I was afraid of failing again. But things never change unless we have the courage to try, so I did, and He is taking the weight off!

There are some things in life you can't change, and therefore must accept. There are other things in life that can be changed. God will help you deal with both.

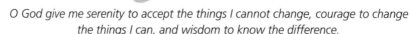

O God give me serenity to accept the things I cannot change, courage to change the things I can, and wisdom to know the difference.
—St. Francis of Assisi

ATTITUDE ADJUSTMENTS

Snap Out of It

Why are you downcast, O my soul? Why so disturbed within me? Put your hope in God, for I will yet praise Him, my Savior and my God.

PSALM 42:11

$\mathcal{D}$id you ever have one of those days where you wake up depressed and can't figure out why? You try to put your finger on the cause. Maybe it's your marriage, kids, job, church, weight, health, finances, house, car, sister, brother, Mother, Father, and on and on. Maybe it's a direct attack from the enemy (shudder), or maybe it's a test from God. The only solution seems to be to pull the covers back over your head and hide from the world.

The cause isn't important, your response is. You can sink down in the clutches of depression, or you can do as David the psalmist did—recognize it, confess it, and declare your hope in God. Encourage yourself with the hope that you will again have reason to praise Him. In fact, don't wait until you *think* you have reason to praise Him. He is your Savior and your God. That's reason enough for your spirit to leap with joy now.

Today's Tip:

Depression comes to us all. Don't dwell on it, but snap yourself out of it with praise.

Put on the ". . . garment of praise instead of the spirit of despair . . ." (Isaiah 61:3). Praise God for who He is, for all He has done in your life, and for all He still plans to do in your future. Put on some good Christian music and sing praises to Him. Dance before Him a dance of praise. Soon that depression will flee and great joy will flood your soul.

God can hear the language of our worry just as clearly as He hears the wailing of our words. And He has promised that He will give us a garment of praise for the spirit of heaviness.
—Jill Briscoe

Seek First His Kingdom

So do not worry, saying, "What shall we eat?" or "What shall we drink?" or "What shall we wear?" For the pagans run after all these things, and your heavenly Father knows that you need them. But seek first His kingdom and His righteousness, and all these things will be given to you as well.

MATTHEW 6:31–34

We like to worry. It gives us something to do. When dieting, we worry about how many calories, fat grams or exchanges are in a particular food. Are we drinking enough water? Are we eating a balance of carbs and proteins? What about our fiber intake? Should we be taking vitamin supplements? Oh, and are we getting enough exercise?

Today's Tip:

Let go and Let God!

What if we stop all that worrying? What if we trust God to tell us when to eat, what to eat and how much to eat? Is your God big enough for all that? Is it possible that by simply relying on our Creator to direct our eating, we could reach our perfect weight without all that fuss? Surely it can't be that simple. But that's just what Weigh Down™ teaches. In fact, if you read the Bible, you will come to the conclusion that God's Word teaches the same thing. That must be where Gwen got the idea!

What should we do with all the spare time we would gain by laying worry aside? Dig into the Word of God. Really get to know the One who loves you so. Get involved with activities that will bring Him glory. Forget about meeting your own needs and start meeting the needs of others. Then watch God take care of you. He will supply all your needs and give you the desires of your heart.

God, who feeds His ravens, will feed His doves. Or, as Matthew Henry puts it, "He that feeds His birds will not starve His babes."
—Charles Spurgeon

ATTITUDE ADJUSTMENTS

Oasis

Your attitude can help or hinder your efforts to lose weight. A positive attitude and a willing spirit will speed you toward achieving your goals in a pleasant frame of mind. A negative attitude and a reluctant spirit will hinder your progress and open the door to defeat.

- What's your attitude toward losing weight?
- Is it mostly positive or negative?
- Are you willing to make the changes God is asking you to make?
- Are you dragging your feet and fighting the process?

Take time to evaluate your current attitude in the space below and write down any changes you intend to make to improve your attitude and ensure your success.

_____

_____

_____

_____

_____

_____

_____

_____

Praise and Reflection

For if I do this thing willingly, I have a reward . . .

I Corinthians 9:17

I Would Be True

"I would be learning day by day the lessons
My heavenly Father gives me in His Word
I would be quick to hear His lightest whisper
And prompt and glad to do the things I've heard
I would be prayerful through each busy moment
I would be constantly in touch with God
I would be tuned to hear His slightest whisper
I would have faith to keep the path Christ trod

HOWARD A. WALTER

Reflection

Do you have a positive attitude toward submission to God?
Be willing to make any necessary attitude adjustments.

Overcoming Temptation

Panting & Drooling

I open my mouth and pant, longing for your commands.

PSALM 119:131

I have a confession to make. I was a cookbook reader. In fact, I enjoyed reading cookbooks more than reading the Bible! This lusting after foods began when I went on my first diet. I would go to the library and check out half-a-dozen cookbooks, rush home and curl up on the sofa and drool over them for hours. I couldn't eat the foods, but I could sure look at them!

I preferred the cookbooks with yummy-looking, color pictures of the finished foods. "Umm, ooh, that looks good!" I would croon. If it looked particularly good, I would read the recipe in detail, mentally blending all the ingredients and "tasting" the finished product. I am sure when the library received the cookbooks back, they made notes on the front inside covers—"Drool marks on page 78" (Chocolate-Mocha Cake), Slobber on page 119 (Country Fried Garlic Chicken).

I rationalized that just looking couldn't make me fat. But I did get fat, because once I started contemplating sin, entertaining myself with thoughts of sin, and tempting myself to sin, the next step was committing the sin! One *can* gain weight from reading cookbooks, and I am living proof!

I was so busy panting and drooling after the food in those cookbooks, that I set myself up for a fall. I should have been panting and drooling after the Word of God.

Today's Tip:

We can protect ourselves from temptation by filling our mind with the Word of God, rather than entertaining ourselves with things that tempt us. So, let's pant after the right thing!

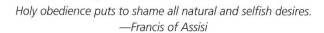

Holy obedience puts to shame all natural and selfish desires.
—Francis of Assisi

OVERCOMING TEMPTATION

Where Does Temptation Come From?

When tempted, no one should say, "God is tempting me." For God cannot be tempted by evil, nor does He tempt anyone, but each one is tempted when, by his own evil desire, he is dragged away and enticed. Then, after desire has conceived, it gives birth to sin; and sin, when it is full-grown, gives birth to death.

JAMES 1:13–15

Consider this scenario:

I woke up this morning, jumped into my Bible study, and promised God to be obedient in my eating today. I rushed off to work with a smile on my lips and good intentions in my heart.

Passing the lunchroom, I smelled fresh coffee brewing. Mmmm—just what I need, I thought, a steaming cup of coffee to start the day right. Woah! Right there, next to the coffeepot, some well-intending co-worker had placed a dozen donuts! No problem, I thought, I'm not hungry. I listened for the growl, just to be sure—no growl. I poured myself a cup of coffee, and while adding the creamer, I glanced at the donuts again. They did look good. It had been a long time since I had a donut. I had not noticed before, but right there on top was my favorite kind—Chocolate cake with Peanut Butter icing! I wasn't going to eat it—I wasn't hungry, but I wondered if they still smelled the same? Glancing around to see if anyone is watching, I lifted it to my nose and breathed deeply. It smelled really good. I could just imagine how it tasted. Was that a growl? I think it was. O.K., maybe I'll just have one donut—and sin was born!

In the past I would have blamed God for tempting me, but after reading this verse and replaying this scenario, I realized that often I allow my own desire to "drag me away" into sin. I just need to learn to control my desires.

Today's Tip:

Don't blame God when temptation strikes you. He does not tempt anyone to sin. We are tempted by Satan and by our own sinful nature.

The Devil only tempts those souls that wish to abandon sin and those that are in a state of grace. The others belong to him; he has no need to tempt them.
—Jean-Baptiste Marie Vianney

It's a Trap

The wicked have set a snare for me . . .

PSALM 119:110A

"No one can eat just one!" (Lays®) "Slam the stack!" (Pringles®) Oh, those wicked commercials! They encourage, entice, and demand us to buy and consume huge quantities of food. They come into our homes and slyly convince us we are hungry. The food looks so appetizing. The people eating the food look so happy and *thin*. And, these snacks are readily available! There's drive-thru windows, convenience stores, and even home delivery! It's all hard to resist.

Think this is just harmless advertising? Consider the millions of dollars that companies pour into television ads each year. They must recover these funds, but how? By making the ads so attractive that you will rush right out and devour their product. They can't afford to leave this to chance, so they spend untold sums researching their target audience to find just the right colors, sounds and glitz to influence you. You are their target—or more accurately, your wallet is their target.

It's a trap! These people are not interested in you, your health, or your happiness. They just want your money, and they will do whatever it takes to get it.

God, on the other hand, cares deeply about you. He wants to see you healthy and happy, and if you allow Him, He will do whatever it takes to give you health and happiness. That may mean resisting the urge to indulge in all that "power eating" that television promotes. If you are going to give in to the influence of another, give in to God— not those advertising executives!

Today's Tip:

As you watch TV, analyze each food commercial you see. Notice the jingles, slogans, pictures they use to tempt you. Being aware of the tactics of temptation make you better equipped to resist them!

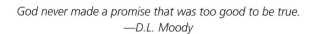

God never made a promise that was too good to be true.
—D.L. Moody

Whose Voice Will Persuade You?

Then the Lord God said to the woman, "What is this you have done?" The woman said, "The serpent deceived me, and I ate." To Adam He said, "Because you listened to your wife and ate from the tree about which I commanded you, You must not eat of it . . ."

GENESIS 3:13,17

*E*ve blamed the serpent, and Adam blamed Eve. Who do you blame when you disobey God?

Fran went to her brother's barbecue with some dread. She knew she would be tempted to overeat. When she arrived, the smell of barbecued chicken simmering over the hot coals took her breath away. "Please help me, God," she pleaded.

When lunch was ready, Fran realized she was not hungry! She whispered a prayer of thanksgiving. As she looked around, she realized that very few people were eating. Fran's brother noticed this and encouraged everyone to dig in. He noticed Fran had not eaten, so he encouraged her to fill a plate. "No thanks, I'm not hungry. I will eat later," was her reply. Repeatedly he urged her to eat and even got a bit angry with her. Finally, out of the fear of offending him, she gave in and ate.

Today's Tip:

Determine ahead of time that you will listen to no voice but God's when you attend social functions that include food.

Eve gave in to the arguments of Satan and ate when God had told her not to eat. Adam, persuaded by his wife, ate against God's wishes. Now, Fran had let another voice influence her to go against God's wishes. She was heartsick. She wept tears of repentance as she drove home.

Become deaf to all voices which persuade you to eat when you are not hungry. Those voices are but disguised temptations of the serpent, himself.

Satan has been called a snake. Better he had been called a chameleon.
For Satan is never quite the same from moment to moment.
—Walter Wink

Look Who's Talking

So I strive always to keep my conscience clear before God and man.

ACTS 24:16

I love the concept of that poor guy who wanders through life with two little beings on his shoulders. An angelic character encourages him to be honorable and good, while the devilish one urges him to just do whatever *feels* good. I've got this whole thing figured out!

The voice that urges you to do what's right (our conscience) is the still, small voice of God. The voice that urges you to go with what feels good is the voice of the devil, whose greatest desire is to keep you from hearing and following the voice of God.

Now, don't think I am getting strange on you, but I hear those voices a lot when it comes to food, don't you? The conversation usually goes something like this:

Today's Tip:

If you hear that little imp in your head, tell him to get lost! Listen to the voice of your conscience—it's really God speaking!

VOICE: "Go ahead, eat. Just a little won't hurt."

ME: "But I'm not hungry, I shouldn't. God would be displeased."

VOICE: "Oh, God doesn't care about such trivial things. Besides, He's the one that put food here for you."

ME: "But He expects me to eat right and take care of my body."

VOICE: "Well, eating just one won't hurt. You can always start again tomorrow."

God blessed us with a conscience. He speaks to us through it, but if we ignore His voice, there's always another voice waiting to steer us in the wrong direction. Keep a clear conscience—always listen to the right voice.

I believe in the living God, and refuse to destroy my conscience.
—Agape (martyr, Greece)

OVERCOMING TEMPTATION

This Means War

For in my inner being I delight in God's law; but I see another law at work in the members of my body, waging war against the law of my mind and making me a prisoner of the law of sin at work within my members. What a wretched man I am! Who will rescue me from the body of death? Thanks be to God—through Jesus Christ our Lord!

ROMANS 7:22–25

We can all relate to the fierce battle described in this passage. We love God. We have a strong desire to keep His laws and to do His will. But, there's another force at work in us—our human nature. Our minds tell us one thing, but our bodies tell us another. My body says I am not hungry, but my mind says it sure would taste good. My body says I've had enough; my desire says just a few more bites. My spirit says read the Word; my eyes say I'm getting sleepy. It's a battle!

There is a war being waged, but it is fought in small daily battles. There's a winner in each skirmish, and the one who wins most will eventually gain the victory. If the spirit controls the body most of the time, we will lead Godly lives and reap eternal rewards. If our human nature is allowed to control our actions more often, then we lose. Our lives will end in destruction, and the enemy will have gained the victory.

Our weapons are mighty. They are prayer, faith, praise, trust, steadfastness, and long-suffering. They are reading the Word of God and believing His promises. God has a mighty army; He is the great general, and the victory has already been won. All He is waiting for is for you to enlist and enjoy the victory with Him.

Today's Tip:

Realize you are in a battle. Determine to let your spirit rule your body. Take advantage of your spiritual weapons and go out there and win one for Christ!

Christianity is a warfare, and Christians spiritual soldiers.
—Robert Southwell

Go To Your Room

When you pray, go into your room, close the door and pray to your Father, who is unseen. Then your Father, who sees what is done in secret, will reward you.

MATTHEW 6:6

"Go to your room, shut the door, and think about what you have done!" I hated those words! Being sent to my room as a child was the worst! We were expected to lie on the bed and do nothing but contemplate the reason for being sent there. There were no video games, stereos, televisions, computers, or telephones in our rooms—just the bed, the dresser, and sheer boredom.

If my parents were lucky, the boredom put us to sleep for a while and gave them some relief, but usually the punishment served its purpose. We lay there staring at the ceiling, listening to the sounds of other children playing outside, and vowed not to repeat our offense if they would ever let us out of that bed! Even 15 minutes of this punishment seemed like hours.

Lately, God has been sending me to my room. Not as a punishment but as a haven. When I am tempted to eat when I am not hungry, God calls me to my room. He is there, waiting for me. I close the door on the temptation and shut myself in with God. As I pray for strength to overcome the pull of sin, there in the quiet of my room, He pours His strength into me. When I leave the room, I have the strength not to repeat the offenses of my past eating habits. I have learned much, and I walk in His strength. Now I just love being sent to my room!

Today's Tip:

When you feel tempted, retreat to your room, pray, and God will meet you there with the strength to overcome the temptation.

We need no wings to go in search of Him, but have only to find a place where we can be alone—and look upon Him present within us.
—Teresa of Avila

Flee the Scene

Flee the evil desires of youth, and pursue righteousness, faith, love and peace, along with those who call on the Lord out of a pure heart.

II TIMOTHY 2:22

"Run, Forrest, Run!" This scene from the movie Forrest Gump reminds me of what we should do when we are facing temptation.

Poor little Forrest had braces on his legs. Every day for years, the same bullies chased him home from school. He couldn't run fast, but he ran. As he ran, the movie depicted the years passing and the braces falling off of Forrest's once weak, thin legs. Years of running from those evil bullies had made him fast and strong.

We must run and flee from evil desires. When the cheesecake is calling your name and your tummy is not hungry—RUN! But don't just run away—run to! Read the verse above again. Notice that God does not just tell us to run in cowardice but to run toward something—to run toward, to *pursue* righteousness, faith, love and peace. He tells us to run along with those who call on the Lord out of a pure heart.

So when you are tempted, run away from the temptation and run toward God. Enlist the help of others who can run along side you. Call a friend and ask them to pray, to advise, even to admonish you. Admit your temptation and ask for their help. That's why we meet in Weigh Down™ groups, so we won't have to run alone. Take advantage of that, and "Run, Forrest, Run!"

Today's Tip:

Next time you are tempted, run, if you can. If you can walk, do so. If that's not possible, run to God in prayer and read the Word. Run to the phone and ask a friend to pray with you. Above all, don't just stand there—run!

He who passively accepts evil is as much involved in it as he who helps to perpetuate it.
—Martin Luther King Jr.

The Full Armor of God

Put on the full armor of God so that you can take your stand against the devil's schemes.

EPHESIANS 6:11

Here's a list of the full armor of God, taken from Ephesians 6:17: Belt of truth, Breastplate of righteousness, Feet fitted with readiness, Shield of faith, Helmet of salvation, Sword of the Spirit.

We are told to put on all the armor, so that we can take our stand against the devil's schemes. The Bible says that our struggle is not against flesh and blood, but against the rulers, against the authorities, against the spiritual forces of evil in the heavenly realms. (Ephesians 6:12)

I know that it is easy to mistake the battle we are in to lose weight as a battle of the flesh. We focus on our body size, the scales, and food and think that we are just fighting a battle with our appetite. On the contrary! This is a spiritual battle we are in. The enemy wants to prevent us from serving God. We want to serve ourselves. God wants us to serve Him. There is a three-way tug of war going on for our spirit that can't be seen with human eyes.

Take advantage of the whole armor of God. Don't just put on one piece and leave yourself partially exposed to the enemy. Hey! Maybe we should wear a "muzzle of obedience" over our mouths when we are not hungry? It's just a thought!

Today's Tip:

Mentally put on the whole armor of God each morning to prepare you for the daily battle. If a piece "slips off" during the day, pick it up and put it back on. Don't forget your muzzle!

I call it an illusion for Christians to seek peace, as though the gospel wanted to make life comfortable for them. The contrary is true. 'I have not come to bring peace on earth, but a sword.' As long as the fight is going on, we have peace only in the fight.
—Christoph Friedrich Blumhardt

OVERCOMING TEMPTATION

Oasis

Are you sitting down? I have something to tell you that might come as a shock. You are not perfect!

If you find you have just overeaten, (and you will) put on your Sherlock Holmes cap, grab your magnifying glass, and go to work. Seek out clues that led up to the "crime." Check out all the usual suspects.

- Family—Did you let someone in the family convince you to overeat? Determine to listen only to God and your body.
- Friends—Do some of your friendships revolve around eating situations? Find new activities to share with your friends, or new friends!
- Circumstances—Did you place yourself in the wrong place at the wrong time? Be prepared for situations which tend to make it easier for you to overeat.
- Emotions—What were you feeling just before you began eating? Determine ahead of time what course of action you will take the next time you feel emotional.

Once you have found the "guilty party," you will be able to protect yourself from being assaulted by them in the future. Temptation can be overcome by some good investigative work. Get busy, Sherlock!

Use the space below to record your "findings."

Praise and Reflection

In the morning will I direct my prayer unto Thee . . .

Psalm 5:3

Did You Think to Pray?

When you met with great temptation
Did you think to pray?
By His dying love and merit
Did you claim the Holy Spirit
As your guide and stay?
When sore trials came upon you
Did you think to pray?
When your soul was bowed in sorrow
Balm of Gilead did you borrow
At the gates of day?

MARY ANN KIDDER

Reflection

Prayer is your greatest weapon in overcoming temptation.
Do you start each day in prayer?

Feasting on the Word

You Can't Satisfy the Monster

Jesus answered, "It is written: Man does not live on bread alone, but on every word that comes from the mouth of God."

MATTHEW 4:4

Remember when you were a child and you thought there was a monster under the bed? Well, there's a monster in my head! It's the Head-Hunger Monster. This creature whispers "I'm hungry!" over and over in my head until I'm convinced I must eat. If I take time to really think about it, I am not usually hungry at all—not truly, stomach-growling hungry.

I may be bored, depressed, anxious, angry, feeling sorry for myself, or any of a dozen other emotions, but I am usually not experiencing the kind of hunger that means my body is calling for fuel. Head-hunger is the spirit's longing to spend time with the Father. Trying to appease this monster with food will only cause it to grow and want more and more, but it will never be satisfied if I feed it the wrong food!

If my stomach is hungry, I can eat and even a small portion will satisfy. But if I feed head-hunger with food, no matter what I eat or how much, it will never be satisfied because food is not what it needs. It needs the Word of God!

Each time you find yourself wandering to the kitchen when you know you are not hungry, grab a spiritual snack instead. Curl up with your Bible. Feed the Head-Hunger Monster with the Word of God and it will turn into a gentle lamb!

Today's Tip:

Why not give that monster a name, like "Clyde." Each time it rears up, say "Down, Clyde!" Then feed him with some spiritual food.

Let us arm ourselves against our spiritual enemies with courage. They think twice about engaging with one who fights boldly.
—John Climacus

God's Snack Food

When your words came, I ate them; they were my joy and my heart's delight, for I bear your name, Oh Lord God Almighty . . .

JEREMIAH 15:16

Is your joy fading fast? Has self-discipline got you down? Cheer up! There is one snack permissible in Weigh Down™ at anytime. You can eat it whether you are hungry or not. You can never eat too much of it, because no matter how much you eat, you will never be stuffed—just thoroughly satisfied. It even comes in different flavors. Some morsels are sweet, some spicy, some sour, and some quite salty.

This snack is God's Word. If you want joy, feast on the Word of God! As Christians, we bear the name of Christ. We are to be imitators of Christ. Therefore, we should be feasting on God's Word to find His will for our lives. It's pretty difficult to follow the Lord's plan for our lives if we never take time to read the instruction book. Eat of it all you want! You may be tempted to gobble it down in huge portions, but let me suggest a better way. Take a tiny bite, savor it, chew on it a while, then after you have pulled every bit of flavor out of it, swallow it. Let your spirit transform the Word into character-changing fuel for your life.

Be warned, however, this snack will make you FAT! Fat in joy, peace, gladness, kindness, contentment, strength, boldness, faith, compassion, love—basically FAT in the Spirit of God. And that's good!

Today's Tip:

Go ahead—get fat in the spirit! Gobble up the Word of God. It will be your joy and your heart's delight!

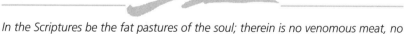

In the Scriptures be the fat pastures of the soul; therein is no venomous meat, no unwholesome thing; they be the very dainty and pure feeding.
—Thomas Cranmer

A Quiet-Time Basket

But Jesus often withdrew to lonely places and prayed.

LUKE 5:16

May I make a suggestion? One of the greatest tools in my Christian growth and in my progress through Weigh Down™ has been my Quiet-Time Basket. It's a beautiful basket lined with lovely fabric and decorated with dried flowers. In this basket is my Bible, my journal, a pen, some 3 X 5 index cards, a packet of note cards and envelopes, and some postage stamps.

Each morning my basket calls me to spend time with God. As I settle in with my coffee and my Bible, I pray that God will direct me in the reading of His Word and will help me see His message for the day. I read until I sense God pointing out something specific, maybe a particular scripture, a characteristic He wants to develop in me, a word of warning about a particular sin, or whatever He chooses to show me. Then I open my journal, date the next blank page, and write what I believe God has shown me. I take time to pray out loud, silently, or in written form in my journal. Sometimes I jot down a great verse on a 3 x 5 card and read it through the day to help hide God's Word in my heart. If I feel prompted, I write a quick note of encouragement to a friend and pop it in the mail.

Now I am ready to face the day. I have God's Word running through my mind, I have committed myself to doing His will, and I am prepared to meet the challenges of the day!

Today's Tip:

Make up your own Quiet-Time Basket. Fill it with everything you might need to settle in with the Lord for a few minutes (or longer) each morning. Any time you feel the need to spend time with God just grab your basket, find a quiet place and settle in.

It is one thing to be told that the Bible has authority because it is divinely inspired, and another thing to feel one's heart leap out and grasp its truth.
—Leslie Weatherhead

Early in the Morning Will I Rise Up and Seek Thee

Morning by morning, O Lord, you hear my voice; morning by morning I lay my requests before you and wait in expectation.

PSALM 5:3

I am not a morning person! Most days, I drag myself out of my comfy bed. I stumble through the house grumbling as my nose leads me to the coffee pot. After pouring myself a cup of hot coffee I head back to the bedroom, where my Bible and journal are waiting for me in my Quiet-Time Basket. I prop the pillows up against the headboard, set my coffee within arms reach, and pick up the Word of God. So begins the best part of my day.

Today's Tip:

This is *our time*—reserved just for me and God. It's the time I draw on God for strength to be obedient throughout the day. It's when I take my will and lay it at His feet and promise to listen for His voice to guide me. I cannot start my morning without this heavenly rendezvous. It's become as vital to me as the air I breathe.

Start your day right. Set an appointment each morning to start the day with the One you love.

It hasn't always been this way. Often, I have rushed into the day without spending time with God. Sometimes I have done it for several days in a row. Suddenly, I'd find myself in the middle of a trying day with little or no strength to face the next crisis. I'd feel totally alone. Then it would dawn on me that I had missed my time with Him.

God longs to spend time with us as much as we need to spend time with Him. It is His desire to fill us each morning with all the love and wisdom we will need to face the day's events. Remember, He is called the Morning Star for a reason!

We ought to see the face of God every morning before we see the face of man.
—D.L. Moody

A Word about Journaling

This is what the Lord, the God of Israel, says: "Write in a book all the words I have spoken to you."

JEREMIAH 30:2

If you have never tried journaling, start today. It has been one of my greatest pleasures in the past few years and a real help in my journey through the "desert" of the Weigh Down™ program.

I use an ordinary steno pad, but there are wonderful new journals on the market today to suit every taste. Each day I turn to a new blank page. As I look at that unblemished page, it reminds me of the day which lays before me. It, too, is fresh and new and waiting to be written on. I date the page and write on it what God teaches me through the day. Sometimes I find myself pouring out my praises to God in the pages of my journal, while on particularly rough days, it is filled with tears of heartache. Between these extremes you will find my laughter at the funny things God shows me and pearls of wisdom that God drops in my heart from time to time.

Today's Tip:

Try journaling for yourself. I am sure it will be a blessing to you.

I love to go back and read where I have been in previous journals. I can see the events of my life unfold there, as well as the victories and failures of my walk with God. Most of all, I can see the hand of God in my life. It reveals a picture of a loving, forgiving God who is continually at work to bring growth into my life.

When I die, I want my daughter to have my journals. They will tell her who her mother was and how God touched her life. Then she can tell my grandchildren. This is my legacy: books filled with the goodness of God.

Poetry is with me, not mechanism but an impulse and a reality, and . . . I know my aims in writing to be pure and directed to that which is true and right.
—Christina Rossetti

Got Milk?

Like newborn babies, crave pure spiritual milk, so that by it you may grow up in your salvation, now that you have tasted that the Lord is good.

I PETER 2:2–3

Milk is great! It nourishes young babies in their first few months of life and gets them off to a great start. A new mother's milk carries all the necessary nutrients to help her baby grow in health. It also carries special immunities to disease to her newborn. But eventually, milk is not enough to keep a baby healthy and growing, and the child must move on to more substantial food. We start with strained foods that are smooth and easy to digest, then toddler foods with chewy morsels, then finally regular foods. Each step helps the baby grow and mature.

I am sure you can see where I am going with this one. As baby (new) Christians, we start out with the milk of the Word and read the easy passages filled with God's promises to care for us, nurture us and protect us. As we grow in the Lord, we should naturally move on to the meatier portions of scripture which challenge us to submit every area of our lives to God. Unfortunately, many Christians never outgrow this stage. They remain stubborn two-year-olds who hold on with both hands to the very thing God asks them to give up, and shout, "Mine!"

Today's Tip:

Be willing to take that next step toward maturity in your relationship with God.

It's hard to move on to the next step, because being an adult is tough. It means taking responsibility for your own actions, suffering to give up your will and yes, even dying to self, but oh, the rewards!

Do not expect the same experience that you had two or twenty years ago. You will have a fresh experience, and God will deal with you in His own way.
—D.L. Moody

Spare Us from the Famine

. . . I will send a famine through the land—not a famine of food or a thirst for water, but a famine of hearing the words of the Lord.

AMOS 8:11

There was a time when the thought of a famine of food and water would have terrified me. I could not go more than an hour or two without eating. If my pantry and refrigerator were not full to the brim, I would panic and rush to the grocery store. I'm not sure if this fear grew out of my gluttony or a teaching early in life that you should always have plenty of food on hand in case someone dropped in at supper time. My mother always cooked in huge quantities. There were 8 in our family, so it took quite a bit of food to feed that many mouths. I never remember a time when company dropped in that there was not enough to feed them. Later in life, I used the "company dropping in" excuse to hoard food.

I have gotten over my obsession to keep my pantry overflowing and the fear of a "famine," but reading this verse sent shivers down my spine. A "famine of hearing the words of the Lord" would be utter destruction for me. I have come to depend so totally on the Word of God to direct my steps, to encourage and correct me, to bring comfort in times of distress, that should I lose the privilege of reading my Bible, I would surely starve spiritually. It's even worse to think of losing that close, one-on-one communication with God through prayer. What if I could no longer hear His sweet voice whisper in my ear?

The only thing that could bring on a famine of this magnitude is disobedience and rebellion against the Lord. I will never let that happen!

Today's Tip:

If you feel the need to hoard food, let it be spiritual food—stock up on the Word of God!

Let the Bible fill the memory, rule the heart and guide the feet.
—Henrietta Mears

Love Letters

How sweet are your promises to my taste, sweeter than honey to my mouth!

PSALM 119:103

Oh, how sweet it is to receive a love letter from the one who holds your heart! Folded neatly and tucked away in my wallet is a letter from my husband. Twenty years have not faded the love that's in that letter. Age does not lessen the way my heart sings each time I unfold its brittle paper and read the love written there.

As I turn the delicate pages of my Bible, I find I am unfolding another beautiful love letter. Between each line is written the love of a Father for His child and the love of a Groom for His bride. Age has not changed its message. Every promise written there He will keep, for He is faithful. He has promised never to leave us nor forsake us and He keeps His Word. He has promised to help us through the storms of life and He will do it. He has asked you to take His hand and walk through life as His bride. Will you accept His offer of love?

Today's Tip:

In the face of such great love, how can we not devote our lives to Him? What is there in this world that is greater than His love? Is there anything that could satisfy me more completely? Surely not anything so trivial as food!

Take time to write God a love letter and take time to read the one He has written you.

The love of food is a poor substitute for the love of God. There is nothing as tasty as the morsels of love served on each page of the Bible. So, go ahead, read the love letter God has written to you. Feel the love pouring out of its pages. Then ask yourself whether anything ever tasted so sweet as the love of God.

I believe the Bible is the best gift God has ever given to men. All the good from the Savior of the world is communicated to us through this book.
—Abraham Lincoln

Just Continue

But as for you, continue in what you have learned . . .

II TIMOTHY 3:14A

𝒯here will be a point when you reach your proper weight. (Honest!) Then, you may wonder, "Now what? Is there a special maintenance plan for Weigh Down™ ? Will I regain my weight?"

In our old days of dieting, once we "went off" the diet, we always regained our weight and then some. You may wonder if that will happen with Weigh Down™. I hate to say this, but it could! It could, that is, if you forget what you have learned about proper eating. It could if you let yourself slip back into your old eating habits. It could if you decide you no longer desire to be obedient to God. It's all up to you!

Today's Tip:

Learn well the principles of Weigh Down™. They will keep you from ever having to worry about your weight again.

The key to maintaining your proper body weight, after you have lost those extra pounds, is the same key you used when you were losing the weight. Remain faithful to God, to the principles of eating as God intended us to eat, and to walking in obedience to Him.

If you are convinced that God loves you and only wants what is best for you, then you won't find it difficult to "continue in what you have learned." You know that God does not deny you good food. You know that overeating is a sin. And your desire is to please God.

As long as you continue doing the things you have learned through the Weigh Down™ program, you need never fear regaining the weight you lost. Just continue!

There must be a beginning of any great matter, but the continuing unto the end until it be thoroughly finished yields the true glory.
—Francis Drake

FEASTING ON THE WORD

Oasis

As you study the Word of God you will find many scripture references to proper eating. These scriptures will inspire you toward obedience, admonish you in your disobedience, reassure you of God's love and often tickle your funny bone! When you find a great scripture that speaks to your heart, jot the references down here so you can refer back to them later.

You can also write the scriptures out on 3 X 5 index cards and store them in your own little "Inspiration Box." Then use them in the following ways:

- Pull one card a day to memorize.
- Stick a card on your refrigerator or bathroom mirror to remind you to be obedient. (Change the cards often so you don't get used to the verse and look right past it.)
- Carry a few of the cards in your purse or car to help you when you are away from home.
- Give a card to a Weigh Down™ buddy to encourage them.

Praise and Reflection

I rejoice at thy Word, as one that findeth great spoil.

Psalm 119:162

Thy Word Is Like a Garden, Lord

Thy Word is like a garden, Lord
With flowers bright and fair
And every one who seeks may pluck
A lovely cluster there
Thy word is like a deep, deep mine
And jewels rich and rare
Are hidden in its mighty depths
For every searcher there.

EDWIN HODDER

Reflection

What fragrant flower or sparkling jewel have you found in God's Word today?

Self-Discipline 101

Keep Me on the Path

Stern discipline awaits him who leaves the path.

PROVERBS 15:10A

God's path to weight loss is straight and well marked—eat when hungry, stop when full. It should be an easy journey, but I have found several obstacles in my path.

Today I tripped on a bump in the road. It was my will. It keeps cropping up from time-to-time, like the stubborn dandelions in my yard. Each time I mow it down, it pops its pretty little head back up through the soil to mock me. Help me, Father, to pluck it out by the roots, so it won't come back.

I've noticed a few potholes labeled *depression* and *self-pity*. If I'm not alert, I may slip into one of these road hazards and waste time as I pull myself out again. Help me to maneuver around these things which threaten to swallow me up, Lord.

There are other people on the road with me. Some are very helpful and encouraging, but others, Lord, seem determined to hinder my progress. "Just one piece won't hurt," they urge, "I made it just for you." "But this is a special occasion," they argue when I say I am not hungry. Help me to block out this road noise and hone in on your voice, God.

There are many attractions along the road which promise to be entertaining and fun, but I know the consequences of leaving the path. Please, Father, set my feet firmly on the path, so that I need not go through "stern discipline."

Today's Tip:

There is so much to learn on the road to thinness. It will help tremendously if you keep in mind that self-discipline saves us from stern discipline!

Discipline puts back in its place that something in us which should serve but wants to rule.
—Carthusians

I Am Torn

Come near to God and He will come near to you. Wash your hands, you sinners, and purify your hearts, you double-minded.

JAMES 4:8

I can't believe how I am struggling today. Part of me is focusing on losing weight and the other part of me really wants to eat huge quantities of food—translation *pig out*. I have been fighting with myself all morning. I wander to the kitchen, open the refrigerator, and ponder all the goodies there. Then I stop, slam the door, and stomp into the living room, angry with myself for wanting to eat. I try to imagine myself slim, then get depressed at how long that might take. What is wrong with me?

I grab my Bible and dig into it like a mad woman. I must find something to take my mind off this tug-of-war. James 4:8 comes into focus. "Come near to God and He will come near to you . . . purify your hearts, you double-minded." I realize that I am double-minded. Part of me wants to be free to indulge myself in all my favorite foods without restraint. While the other part wants to eat to please God and to lose weight. I must decide today whether to devote myself to food or to God. Until I make that decision, I will never be free of this conflict in my heart. I made my decision.

I get up, go to the bathroom sink, and wash my hands as a symbolic gesture of the decision I have just made to purify my heart and become single-minded in my devotion and obedience to God.

Today's Tip:

If you are caught in this tug-of-war between food and obedience to God, consider the truth of this verse. Do you need to "wash your hands"?

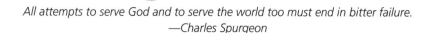

All attempts to serve God and to serve the world too must end in bitter failure.
—Charles Spurgeon

Oh, Grow Up!

Like newborn babies, crave pure spiritual milk so that by it you may grow up in your salvation, now that you have tasted that the Lord is good.
                                                                I PETER 2:2–3

Have you ever been in the grocery store checkout line and overheard a child who wants his mother to buy him candy? First he asks, then he demands, then he whines, then he cries, and then he screams! I don't know about you, but I want the mother to discipline him—forcefully! To my dismay, more times than not, the mother will cave in to the little tyrant. Now, what good has she done the child? She has not taught him respect, discipline, or obedience, but self-indulgence, to demand his own way, and to ignore those in authority.

Are we like that with God? Are we self-centered children who demand our own way, then spoil ourselves by giving in to our every whim? The whole goal of this (Weigh Down™) and all of God's teaching is to transform us from spoiled, self-indulgent children who insist on our own way, to mature, obedient sons & daughters who prefer the Father's will over our own. He is molding us into the image of His Son who only did the Father's will.

Our self-indulgence spreads to all areas of our lives but is most evident in the area of food. Christians have allowed overeating to become the only "socially acceptable" sin in the church. Self-indulgence to the point of self-destruction is sinful, even if it is overlooked by the church today. Right is right and wrong is wrong—even if the whole world overeats. We are accountable to God, not man.

Today's Tip:

Listen for that spoiled child today. When it starts demanding its own way, a little discipline is in order!

Without disciplining the body, focusing the mind, purifying the emotions, and controlling the will no one can hear the sound of Truth or see the vision of God.
—Stanley J. Samartha

Ouch!

And if your right hand causes you to sin, cut it off and throw it away. It is better for you to lose one part of your body than for your whole body to go into hell.

MATTHEW 5:30

Sometimes God can be so dramatic! I tried to imagine cutting off my own right hand (the one that always reaches for the potato chips) and throwing it away. What a gruesome thought! Then I gave this verse a bit more consideration.

It's not really my body that causes me to overeat. My hand does not act on its own when it reaches for second and third helpings. My mouth does not independently chew mounds of food. My *brain* does not even make the decision to over-indulge in food. The real culprit here is my will. It's my stubborn will that insists on having its own way, in spite of what I know will be pleasing to God. It's my will that rebels against submission to the Father in any area of self-control.

We must put to death our will if we are to keep ourselves from disobedience, for it is our will which gets in the way of committing ourselves to a life submitted to Jesus Christ and to doing His will above ours. Unfortunately, man's will has the ability to resurrect itself. We must continually be watchful and put to death our will each time it threatens to pull us into sin. It would be much better to lose our will than to risk our soul going to hell!

Today's Tip:

Put to death that part of your will, which rises up against the Father.

After we have made our requests known to Him our language should be, "Thy will be done." I would a thousand times rather that God's will should be done than my own.
—D.L. Moody

Keep the Covenant

I will not violate my covenant or alter what my lips have uttered.

PSALM 89:34

God keeps His promises, and He expects us to do the same. How many times have you said you were not going to overeat, and yet you did? O.K., maybe you are not like me, maybe you always do what you say you are going to do, but I admit to having a problem in this area.

My daughter knew this, so when she was young and I told her we would do something fun—a movie, skating, a trip to the mall—she would say, "You promise?" She knew that if she could squeeze a promise out of me, that I would follow through. If I didn't promise, then I could hedge my way out of it. "Well, I meant it, but Mom's tired now, maybe another day." Or "I meant it, but I thought we would have the money, and it didn't come in." I'm embarrassed to admit it, but that's the way I was.

Today's Tip:

Make it a point to keep your word. If you said it, do it.

I have learned the importance of keeping my word. I make it my goal to do what I say I will do, even if I don't feel like doing it when the time comes. It's critical that we teach our children the value of keeping our word. It's even more important that we keep our promises to God. Don't make a promise to God that you won't keep. Be sure you don't "alter what your lips have uttered." If God is faithful in keeping His promises to us, we should do the same.

Apply this to your eating. If you say you are not going to eat until you are hungry, don't eat. If you intend to eat just one cookie, do it. God hears the promises of the heart, as well as the spoken promise.

Those who are quick to promise are generally slow to perform.
—Charles Spurgeon

Just Do It!

Do not merely listen to the Word, and so deceive yourselves. Do what it says. Anyone who listens to the Word but does not do what it says is like a man who looks at his face in a mirror and, after looking at himself, goes away and immediately forgets what he looks like. But the man who looks intently into the perfect law that gives freedom, and continues to do this, not forgetting what he has heard, but doing it — he will be blessed in what he does.

JAMES 1:22–25

It won't work if you don't do it! God's principles are true and life-changing, whether you apply them to overeating or any other problem in life. But they will not work unless you do them! Just knowing God's will is not enough — it must be applied to your life in order for you to benefit from it, in order for you to please God.

I look in the mirror. Many times, I am not happy with what I see there. I do not like my body's shape, which is the result of overeating. I don't like the spiritual weakness which is a result of my disobedience to the Father. I make promises to God, but just hours later I have forgotten what I look like. I find myself doing the very things that caused my reflection in the mirror to be so unpleasant to my eyes.

It's time to look in the mirror. Really look. Are you doing all you have learned about God's way of eating? Are you waiting for hunger and stopping when full? Are you studying God's word on a daily basis? Are you submitting your will to Him? Be brutally honest with yourself. Are you doing what God wants you to do?

Today's Tip:

Remember, the perfect law (God's law) gives freedom, and the man who continues in it, not forgetting what he has heard but doing it, will be blessed in what he does.

A Christianity which does not prove its worth in practice degenerates into dry scholasticism and idle talk.
—Abraham Kuyper

It Gets Easier

And the God of all grace, who called you to His eternal glory in Christ, after you have suffered a little while, will Himself restore you and make you strong, firm and steadfast.

I PETER 5:10

Self-control brings suffering. Don't let anyone tell you anything different. In the beginning, it was a continual battle for me to push away from food. It was agony to wait until I was truly hungry before I could eat. I was grouchy most of the time and pouted a lot. A life-long devotion to food is a tough habit to break. I have good news for you, however. The suffering only lasts a little while. If you are being consistently obedient, then you will get stronger, and it will become easier to control your eating.

Today's Tip:

Are you prolonging your suffering, by divided devotion? Decide this day whom you will serve.

If you are not careful, however, you can prolong your suffering. If you bounce back and forth between self-control and self-indulgence, between your love for God and your love for food, the suffering will continue. It is painful to be torn between two loves. You can make this much more difficult than it needs to be, or you can make it easy.

Once you make the commitment to steadfastly choose obedience over rebellion, an incredible thing happens. God makes you stronger and firmer in your resolve to overcome the temptation to overeat. It gets easier to say no to food when you are not hungry. It's easier to recognize when you have had enough food and stop eating. The suffering stops, and it is replaced by the great joy that comes with obedience.

The more consistent you are in obedience, the quicker the suffering ends and victory begins. Let God shorten your suffering. Consistently surrender your will to Him today and start walking in victory.

When God is going to do a wonderful thing. He begins with a difficulty.
—Charles Inwood

Oasis

It's going to take some retraining to break old habits. We must discipline ourselves to react differently to food than we have in the past. If I find myself wanting to eat when I am not hungry, I try to immediately get involved in some other activity to take my mind off food. Here are some alternatives to eating I have used.

- Read the Bible.
- Call a friend.
- Take a bath.
- Do some housework.
- Take a walk.

List below some activities you can do to distract yourself when you are not hungry, but want to eat.

_____

_____

_____

_____

_____

_____

_____

Praise and Reflection

I determined not to know anything . . . save Jesus Christ.

I Corinthians 2:2

I Am Resolved

I am resolved no longer to linger
Charmed by the world's delight
Things that are higher, things that are nobler
These have allured my sight
I am resolved to follow the Savior
Faithful and true each day
Heed what He sayeth, do what He willeth
He is the living way
I am resolved to enter the kingdom
Leaving the paths of sin
Friends may oppose me, foes may beset me
Still I will enter in

PALMER HARTSOUGH

Reflection

What resolves are you making in the area of self-discipline?

Let's Be Honest

Time to Face the Music

Therefore to him that knoweth to do good, and doeth it not, to him it is sin.

JAMES 4:17 (KJV)

Overeating is sin. There—I said it! For years I admitted that overeating made me uncomfortable, unattractive, and unhealthy, but I would not admit that it was sin. After all, God put food here. He gave us taste buds to enjoy the food. He created our bodies to require food. So how could eating be sinful?

It's not! Food is not sinful, but *the love of food* is, if we allow that love to win out over what we know to be the will of God. Most Christians will admit that we must care for our bodies. We will say that the use (or overuse) of harmful substances such as tobacco, drugs, or alcohol is sinful. Deliberately bringing harm to our bodies would quickly be proclaimed sin in the Christian community, yet we overlook the damaging effects of overeating.

God had taken a back seat in my heart when it came to food. I knew He wanted me to be self-controlled, but I allowed food to control me. It was the one thing I couldn't seem to surrender to God. It didn't seem so bad until I read this scripture:

"For if you live according to the sinful nature, you will die; but if by the Spirit you put to death the misdeeds of the body, you will live." Romans 8:13

If we know that controlling our appetites is God's will and yet we don't do it, it is sin. And if we allow ourselves to continue to live according to our sinful nature, we will die.

I believe this scripture is speaking of spiritual death. That's too high a price for me to pay. How about you?

Today's Tip:

Time to get honest with God. If you allow your love for food to keep you from doing what you know is right, pray for His forgiveness and start over.

All I can do is to try to be honest—honest to God and about God.
—John A.T. Robinson

What Excites You?

For out of the abundance of the heart, the mouth speaks.

LUKE 6:45B

You can tell a lot about a person by their voice, not the words they say, but their tone of voice.

I have a dear friend who taught me a powerful lesson, although she does not know it. We were talking on the phone, which we do often. We discuss everything from our families to our jobs, and I enjoy talking with her. But I noticed something today. Almost every time we talk, the conversation eventually turns to food.

She will launch into a detailed description of a new recipe she found. She lists all the ingredients, the perfect seasonings to use, just how to chop the vegetables, how to sauté the meat, which side dishes to serve with it, every detail. As she speaks, her voice rises in pitch just a bit. Her words come faster, and her excitement is evident.

No other topic of conversation we have ever discussed has elicited this kind of response in her voice, including our long conversations about the Lord! I realized today, that my friend is in *love* with food. She is also extremely overweight and longs to be in control of her eating. I don't think that will happen until she transfers her love of food over to God.

I'm praying for God to give me an opportunity to share with her His perfect plan for eating and weight loss. I want to tell her how He is transforming my love for food into an ever-deepening relationship with Him. I want her to know that God can and will do the same for her, if she will give Him a chance. I bet when I tell her, she will hear the excitement in my voice!

Today's Tip:

Listen to your own voice. What causes your voice to reflect excitement? This is a good indicator of what you love. Is it God that excites you—or food?

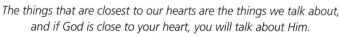

The things that are closest to our hearts are the things we talk about, and if God is close to your heart, you will talk about Him.
—A.W. Tozer

Don't Deceive Yourself

If anyone considers himself religious and yet does not keep a tight rein on his tongue, he deceives himself and his religion is worthless.

JAMES 1:26

The principle of this verse goes beyond the words we speak. It speaks of the value God places on self-control. He expects His children to take control of all their actions. Today, it's common practice to blame others for our actions. Many say "I had a hard childhood." "My mother was an alcoholic." "Children ridiculed me when I was little." "My whole family is overweight." While it is true that life is difficult, and there are many hurts along the way, God will not allow you to use them to excuse your disobedience.

Here are some overeating excuses I have used:

Today's Tip:

Write down the excuses you are using, then take control of your actions.

Occasions—Vacation, Party, Buffet, Wedding, Thanksgiving, Barbecue

Circumstances—House guests, Was off schedule, Dinner with friends

Emotions—Anger, Worry, Depression, Loneliness, Boredom

Here are some disobedience excuses I have used:

I slipped—I didn't "slip" into disobedience, I chose to disobey
I forgot—I did not "forget," I chose to disobey
I can't—I can be obedient. *I can't*, properly translated, would be *I won't!*
I'll try—"Try" leaves an open window for disobedience

If you have used some of these same excuses, get honest with yourself and with God. Say, "I was disobedient." Repent. Better yet, practice a little more self-control, and there will be no need for excuses or repentance, just rejoicing!

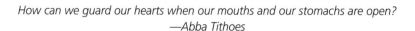

How can we guard our hearts when our mouths and our stomachs are open?
—Abba Tithoes

Fill in the Blank

But they all alike began to make excuses . . .

LUKE 14:18

If it weren't for _____, I could lose weight. How would you fill in the blank? Your husband, your boss, your genes, your upbringing, your weak will, your love for chocolate . . . what?

I have used a thousand excuses for why I couldn't lose weight, and all of them are lame. To tell the truth there's only one way to fill in that blank—"If it weren't for *my overeating*, I could lose weight." That's it—nothing else keeps us fat but eating too much food. It's not our mothers or our metabolism—it's our choice to chew and chew and chew!

So, why do we continue to overeat when we so desperately want to lose weight? We really need to sit down and look at why we insist on stuffing our bodies with food it does not need. What is it that keeps us running to food instead of to God? Self-examination is a necessary and often painful step in losing weight, but God is there to help us, even with this. Once we take a good long look at what makes us keep eating, we can turn this over to the Lord, and let Him be our source of comfort—not the food.

Let's stop making excuses. Overeating is a conscious choice we make. But, why do we continue to make a choice that makes us so unhappy? Being honest with ourselves is the first step to allowing God to reign in this area of our lives.

Today's Tip:

Next time you overeat, grab a piece of paper and write down what you were feeling just before you overate. Think about it for a while. Then commit yourself to go to God the next time you feel this same way. See if you don't feel much better when comforted by God, instead of food.

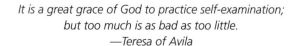

It is a great grace of God to practice self-examination;
but too much is as bad as too little.
—Teresa of Avila

A Mouth Full of Gravel

Food gained by fraud tastes sweet to a man, but he ends up with a mouth full of gravel!

PROVERBS 20:17

Sometimes it's so easy to pull the wool over my own eyes! I believe that I am following God's plan for eating when I am only half-heartedly doing so. I can convince myself that I am truly experiencing hunger just about the time I remember I have a piece of carrot cake left in the refrigerator.

Then, when my weight loss comes to a standstill I whine about my "plateau." I'll complain, "I don't understand! I'm following the Weigh Down™ program, why am I not losing?" FRAUD!

I have spent years deceiving myself about why I have a weight problem. It's time to face the truth. A dishonest gain of food would be fraud. If I ate when I said I wouldn't, or if I claimed I had been obedient and had really not, it's fraud. If I say my heart wants to please God, but my actions (eating) prove that just the opposite is true, it's fraud.

The food may taste sweet when eaten in fraud, but the consequences of disobedience would be as awful as walking around with a mouth full of gravel! Prayer becomes difficult when you know in your heart that you have not been honest with God. It's hard to talk to the Father with a mouth full of gravel!

Today's Tip:

Go outside and find a small piece of gravel. Carry it in your pocket as a reminder to be honest with God and yourself where your eating is concerned.

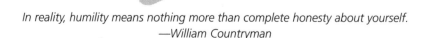

In reality, humility means nothing more than complete honesty about yourself.
—William Countryman

I've Got a Secret

You have set our iniquities before you, our secret sins in the light of your presence.

PSALM 90: 8

Remember that old television show, "I've Got a Secret"? The host would bring on a guest who had some strange hobby or occupation like a man who collected nose hairs or the guy who invented the paper clip. A panel of experts would ask questions until they narrowed it down, and then they would write down a guess at the "secret" of the guest.

I thought about what it would have been like for me to go on that show. I wonder if the panel could have guessed all my "secret" eating? No one else had. My family and friends had no idea that I could eat six Nutty Buddy ice cream cones in a row. My husband did not know that after he fell asleep on the couch that I could eat a whole bag of potato chips. At least I don't think they knew— but I bet just one look at my ballooning body would have given them a hint.

Today's Tip:

Don't think you are keeping any secrets from God. He sees and wants to help. Let Him.

Secret bingeing is common among overeaters. I don't know if I thought that food eaten in secret didn't *count*, or if I was just so ashamed of how much food I was eating that I didn't want anyone to see me. It's highly possible that I was just so stingy that I ate in secret so I didn't have to share!

I guess I forgot that there are no secrets from God. The light of His presence shines brightly on our hearts and nothing is hidden from Him. He sees the binges, He sees the stolen bites, and He sees the deceit of our heart. If you are still eating in "secret," stop. Come clean before the Lord. He already knows and waits for you to be honest with Him and ask for His help.

God and our conscience know our secrets. Let them correct them.
—Mark the Ascetic

But Lord, This Is Too Hard

Now what I am commanding you today is not too difficult for you . . .

DEUTERONOMY 30:11

A question in my Weigh Down™ workbook asked: What about this program are you finding too difficult?

I was ready for that question! I had so many answers that I doubted they would all fit on the few lines provided. I had been struggling for the last few days. It seemed I was always hungry, and recognizing I was full only happened 15 minutes after I had eaten way too much! The scale was going the wrong way, and my mood was getting ugly.

Then I saw that tiny little word right in the middle of that question. My pen halted in mid-air when I saw the word—"too." If they had just asked, "What about this program are you finding difficult?" I could have written:

Today's Tip:

When things seem too difficult ask—Is it the program or your will?

Waiting for hunger, stopping before stuffed, giving up my will, explaining it to my friends, being patient with slow weight loss, and on and on and on . . .

But, there it was, glaring at me. It said "too" difficult, meaning so difficult that it couldn't be done, impossible. I had to admit that nothing about the Weigh Down™ program was too difficult. The problem was not with the program but with my heart. I still wanted to do my own thing when it came to eating. The problem was submitting my will to God.

Once again I find myself facing a little self-examination. Time to strip away some dishonesty. Time to admit that the only difficult part of eating according to God's plan is breaking years of self-indulgent behavior. It's not the program that's difficult—it's *unspoiling* me!

All thing are possible to one who believes.
—Bernard of Clairvaux

Are We Deceiving Ourselves?

If we claim to be without sin, we deceive ourselves and the truth is not in us. If we confess our sins, He is faithful and just and will forgive us our sins and purify us from all unrighteousness.

I JOHN 1:8–9

I read a letter today from a Weigh Down™ participant that shocked me. This lady has been in Weigh Down™ groups for 2 years and has not lost one pound off her 250-pound body! She lamented the lack of weight loss and assured me that she has followed the program faithfully. She said she has drawn closer to God than ever before and that she is listening to His voice, but that it has not affected her weight.

How would I politely tell this dear lady that I think she has deceived herself? She can't possibly be following the program or be walking in obedience to God in her eating. God would not tell her to continue to eat amounts of food that would maintain her overweight body. If she would refrain from eating until she was truly hungry and would listen for God to tell her when to stop, she would lose weight. God's plan works!

God used this woman's letter to cause me to examine my eating. Have I been fully obedient, as I thought, or have I deceived myself as well? My weight loss has slowed down a bit and sometimes it stands still. I tell myself I am doing my part, but now I wonder. I intend to be more diligent in eating only when I hear a growl and to stopping as soon as I feel prompted by God. No more self-deceit!

Today's Tip:

If your weight has remained at a plateau for sometime, ask yourself if you are truly being obedient. If not, confess and receive His forgiveness.

Of all forms of deception self-deception is the most deadly, and of all deceived persons the self-deceived are the least likely to discover the fraud.
—W. Tozer

What's Your Motivation?

. . . was it really for me that you fasted? And when you were eating and drinking, were you not just feasting for yourselves?

ZECHARIAH 7:5B–6

God asked these questions of the people and priests of Israel thousands of years ago, but He is still asking the same question today—"What is your motivation for what you do in my name?"

Whether we fast or eat, God looks beyond our words and our actions into our hearts to find the true motivation behind what we do. Many times I fasted (dieted), not to be obedient to God, but for vanity's sake. I wanted to be thin, to wear flashy clothes, to attract attention, to feel superior. Other times, I would join in a Thanksgiving feast or a Christmas dinner to celebrate the goodness of God. But, my thoughts were focused on the food and far from God.

Today's Tip:

Make a list of the reasons you want to lose weight. Ask God to make your motivations clear to you, then pray about what you find hidden in your heart.

He may very well have asked this question of me, and I think He still does. I must still examine my motivation for the way I eat. If I hope to overcome this pull of food on my life, I must rid my heart of any hidden agenda concerning food. I must have a pure desire to eat only to please God—whether I am eating or refraining from eating.

Any time you are doing something "for the Lord," examine your heart for the true motivations behind your activities. The Lord loves and honors a pure heart, one free from self-deception. Why do you do what you do?

In the fulfillment of your duties, let your intentions be so pure that you reject from your actions any other motive than the glory of God and the salvation of souls.
—Angela Merici

Oasis

If you really want to be free from overeating, you are going to have to take a good long look at the condition of your heart. You must be totally honest with yourself and with God about why you overeat and why you rebel against Him. Self-examination can be painful, but without it, you will not discover the hidden motives that keep you overweight and disobedient to God.

The wonderful news is that God will not condemn you, no matter what you discover. He already knows your heart and longs to free you from the things that are holding you back. As you honestly seek to understand yourself, confess any sin you find in your life, ask God to forgive you, and be willing to make changes that will help you grow spiritually. Record your discoveries and the changes you plan to make here.

Today's Tip:

Praise and Reflection

Sell all that thou hast…and come, follow me.

Luke 18:22

Nothing Between

Nothing between my soul and the Savior
Naught of this world's delusive dream
I have renounced all sinful pleasures
Jesus is mine, there's nothing between
Nothing between like worldly pleasure
Habits of life though harmless they seem
Must not my heart from Him e'er sever
He is my all, there's nothing between

C. ALBERT TINDLEY

Reflection

Let's be honest.
Is there anything standing between you and God?

Let's Get Practical

Open Wide

I am the Lord your God, who brought you up out of Egypt. Open wide your mouth and I will fill it.

PSALM 81:10

From birth, children instinctively know the proper way to eat. They cry for food when hungry and will not eat beyond full unless forced to do so. They don't cry for food when they are wet—they cry to be changed. They don't want food for any reason other than hunger.

We quickly short-circuit their instincts. We wiggle the bottle in their mouths to get them to finish that last ounce of formula. We wake them from their sleep because the clock says it's time for their next feeding. We play games to force them to finish their meals—remember the airplane that flew around, bringing them those last few morsels? We teach them that food is the cure all. When they get hurt, angry, too active or bothersome, we give them food to appease them. "Here, honey, have a cookie. It will be all better." They grow older and we become "Clean Your Plate" Moms. "You can't have dessert until you clean your plate." "Clean your plate, there are starving children in China, Cambodia, Indonesia . . ." "Be a big girl (boy), clean your plate."

Today's Tip:

If you still have children at home, help them get back to eating God's way.

And our children got big. The number of obese children in the United States is astounding. We have short-circuited their God-given ability to know their "hungry and full" signals, and they will have to suffer through the same battle with weight that we are now fighting.

God is a loving parent. He wants us to "open wide." He will feed us when hungry yet not beyond full. Let's get back in touch with our God-given instincts for proper eating. Eat when hungry, stop when full, and use food only to refuel your body. Let God meet every other need.

One of our greatest tasks is to demonstrate to the young people of this generation that there is nothing stupid about righteousness.
—A.W. Tozer

LET'S GET PRACTICAL

Enjoy Good Food—In Moderation

In the house of the wise are stores of choice food and oil, but a foolish man devours all he has.

PROVERBS 21:20

Remember the days just before you started a new diet? Your first step was to get all of the "good stuff" out of the house. Of course, to do this you almost always ate all the "good stuff."

Next came the trip to the grocery store. You felt so righteous pushing your cart full of lettuce, carrots, cottage cheese, tuna, and rice cakes. True, it took you twice as long to shop, due to all that label reading. You will have to admit you felt a bit of resentment as you read the labels on your favorite foods, only to have to put them back on the shelf because they were "over the limit." I know you gasped as the register cha-chinged a total much higher than usual. But, you had bought Fat-Free, Sugar-Free, Taste-Free everything, and you were headed toward "skinny"!

Today's Tip:

Enjoy your favorite foods, eaten in moderation and obedience.

Did all that effort pay off? No. After a week of eating diet foods, you were feeling deprived. All you could think of were the foods you were craving—normal foods. In frustration, you ran right out and binged at the nearest fast-food restaurant. You chucked the diet and restocked your pantry, pushing all that "righteous" food to the back of the shelf until your next diet. So, what are you supposed to do now?

Look at the verse again. Notice that it says a wise man has stores of choice foods and (listen-up) OIL! There's nothing wrong with having delicious foods in your house. The problem comes when we foolishly devour all we have—usually at one sitting! We just need to practice some self-control. Eat what you like, but only between the boundaries of hungry and satisfied. The weight might come off slower, but it will be permanent.

Where there is measure and proper blend,
there is nothing too much or too little.
—Augustine of Hippo

Everything Is Permissable, But . . .

Everything is permissible for me—but not everything is beneficial. Everything is permissible for me, but I will not be mastered by anything.

I CORINTHIANS 6:12

I've learned that no food is "good" or "bad." All food is created by God, and He pronounced it all good. Refraining from eating certain foods which contain sugar or fat will not make you more righteous, nor will eating diet foods, vegetables, low-fat or low-sugar foods. God permits us to eat all foods without guilt.

But, even though all food is permissible, for some people, not all food is beneficial. I have diabetes. In time, as I lose my excess weight, I am sure the diabetes will go away (according to my doctor). Until that time, though, it is not beneficial for me to eat lots of sugary foods. I lost sight of this fact after joining Weigh Down™ and experiencing the freedom to eat whatever I wanted. I started choosing sugary foods that made it more difficult to control my blood sugar. I have had to cut back on sweets.

For each of us, it will be different. Some will need to watch their fat intake until their cholesterol problem is under control. Some will have to limit sodium in their diet until their blood pressure is in check. Some will need to eliminate a particular food until they are in control, because that food "masters" them.

I believe God's ultimate plan is to allow us to enjoy all foods, but due to the strain we have put on our bodies by overeating, it may be wise to seek Him for which foods are most beneficial to us, then enjoy!

Today's Tip:

Ask God to show you not only which foods are permissible, but which would be most beneficial to you at this time.

God in His great mercy decides what is best for each one.
—Cloud of Unknowing (Book on the spiritual life)

Give Me My Portion

Feed me with the food that is my portion.

PROVERBS 30:8B (NASB)

I grew up in a large family. Mom and Dad didn't have much money for food treats, so anytime "goodies" came into the house, there was a mad scramble to get our portion before it was all gone. There was always the hope that you would get just a little bit more than the next kid, or that you could wheedle, bribe or cajole some of theirs away from them. "Mom, he got more than me!" was a familiar cry around our house. Poor Mother had to assume the role of "Portion Police" each time a treat was brought to the table.

Some habits are hard to break. I still find myself rushing to eat goodies when they enter the house. I would love to use the excuse that I have to *grab quick* or the children will eat it all, but I only have one child and she left home 9 years ago! I have no excuse, but I still find myself comparing the size of the pork chops to see which I will take for myself and which one I will leave for my hubby. I still snatch the "last one" from the package, not because I am hungry, but because it's "the last one."

Father, forgive me. Please, feed me with the food that is *my* portion. Not *more* than my portion, not *someone else's* portion, but the food that is my portion, and I shall be content! At those times I want to eat more than I should, You, O Lord, are my portion! I will feast on your Word for,

"You are my portion, Oh Lord; I have promised to obey your words." Psalm 119:57

Today's Tip:

Consider the portion-size you put on your plate. If God were filling your plate, what size portion would He place there?

Heaven will be the endless portion of every man who has heaven in his soul.
—Henry Ward Beecher

Less Is Better

Better the little that the righteous have than the wealth of many wicked.

PSALM 37:16

I have made a startling discovery. A little food tastes much better than a lot of food! Have you ever noticed that the first few bites of food are the best? Your taste buds are alive with the sensations of each flavor, but after a while, your taste buds lose their sensitivity and the exquisite flavor turns mundane.

Try it yourself. Next time you're hungry, notice how good the food tastes at first, then notice when it begins to taste just so-so. If you continue eating that same food, eventually you will lose your taste for it. Eating another bite will seem disgusting. I discovered this phenomenon by overeating (I admit it) my favorite dessert, carrot cake. I would never have imagined that carrot cake would not taste good to me, but by the end of the piece, I was almost sick. What tasted so wonderful just a few minutes before, now had a sickening, sweet taste. I actually had to force myself to finish the last of it. What a goofy thing to do!

Today's Tip:

Go ahead, try it yourself. Do the "Taste Bud Test."

Fortunately, I have discovered another startling fact. Once you allow yourself to become hungry again, your taste buds return to normal and food once again tastes great, even the same food that tasted awful when you overate it. I still like carrot cake — in moderation, of course.

I've been using this to gauge when to stop eating. When the food stops tasting exquisite and starts tasting just so-so, I stop. I can always eat more later when I get hungry, and this way eating is always a real pleasure. Just one more way God has shown me to listen to my body.

From all slavish habits and excess we must abstain,
and touch what is set before us in a decorous way.
—Clement of Alexandria

Look Up from Your Plate

I lift up my eyes to the hills—where does my help come from?

PSALM 121:1

Life goes on all around me while I eat! Now, this might not be news to you, but it was a real revelation to me. For years, I would sit down to a meal and never take my eyes off the plate until it was empty. I had no idea what was going on around me.

Many families use mealtime to catch up on each other's daily activities. They laugh and share as they eat. In our family, mealtime was for eating. I'm sure between my five brothers and I, we drove our parents crazy with bickering and horseplay at the table. Finally they would insist on silence. I don't blame them; it's hard to enjoy a meal amid all that chaos, but I think this is where the notion of focusing on my plate came from. I didn't want to risk being sent from the table and missing out on the food (heaven forbid!), so I just kept my eyes on my plate and cleaned 'er up!

Today's Tip:

Look up! God has provided many things to help take your focus off food.

I have recently discovered that conversation greatly enhances a meal. My husband and I now use this time to catch up, to talk about our goals, and to laugh together. I have learned to put my fork down, take time to look around, sip my water, and join in the pleasures of dining. I find I am not eating as much. My food even seems to digest better. Slowing down as I eat helps me to recognize when I have had enough food. I don't mind stopping before my plate is clean, because I have other things to do at the table besides eat. I've gone from just eating to *dining*. It's a whole new experience, and I love it!

I do not want to make eating an occupation, but something accessory.
—Abba Pior

My Top of the Hour Technique

Could you not keep watch for one hour? Watch and pray so that you will not fall into temptation. The spirit is willing but the flesh is weak.

MARK 14:37B–38

How many times have you heard these words? "You didn't put on all this weight overnight, so you can't expect to lose it overnight." I have heard them many times and I hate them!

I know it's going to take months of eating right to lose all of my extra weight, but I can't imagine going for months without overeating. I have never been able to do it before, so it seems almost impossible. It's too overwhelming for me to think about months of self-control. But, I have discovered if I think about those months in smaller increments, it seems much more manageable. Even weeks or days seem too big for me, but I can handle *hours*!

Today's Tip:

Try my Top of the Hour Technique today. What if you fail during one hour? Start again at the "Top of the Hour"!

If looking at a whole day of eating right seems too huge for you, you might want to try my "Top of the Hour Technique." At the top of each hour tell God, out loud, whether you intend to be obedient to Him with your eating for the next hour. Chances are you will be unable to say, "You know, God, I have been so good for the last 3 hours that I have decided to be disobedient to you during the next hour."

Chances are even greater that you will choose to say, "Father, I commit to be obedient to you in my eating for the next hour," and because you have made that commitment, you will keep your word. When you add up all those obedient hours, you will find that being faithful in hours has made you faithful in days, weeks, months, years, and finally in life!

My hour will come, when it is His hour.
—William Q. Lash (Will Quinlan)

Nighttime Curfew

In the night I remember your name, O Lord, and I will keep your law.
PSALM 119:55

Okay, that's it, no more late night munchies! Each evening from 9:00 until my 11:00 bedtime, I struggle with eating. I have dinner at about 5:00, so I often do get hungry before bedtime, but I have a definite problem with control in those evening hours. If I would just get a small snack, I would be fine. That would carry me through until morning, but I don't do that. I get something sweet, then I need something salty, then maybe something spicy, and on and on. It's a cycle I have not broken.

Notice, I did not say it's a cycle I *can't* break, or *haven't been able* to break, but that I *have not* broken. I haven't even really tried. I've grieved over it. I've been sorry that I overeat at night. I have wished that I would quit doing it. But, I haven't taken responsibility for my own actions. I am capable of controlling myself; I just have not done so. This is obviously an area that I need to submit to God.

I am imposing a curfew on myself. I will not eat after 9:00 p.m. This might seem drastic (at least to me), but sometimes we must take drastic measures to discipline our self-indulging nature. Because I have not been able to *control* my nighttime eating, I will simply *abstain* from it. I will not be ruled by my fleshly desires. Food will not control me. I have a stubborn will, but if I use that will to be stubbornly committed to obedience to God, I can turn this thing around.

In the night, I will remember the Lord, and I will keep His laws! Anyone else have this same problem? I invite you to join me in my nighttime curfew.

Today's Tip:

Use your stubborn will to your advantage. Determine to make it serve God.

There is no pillow so soft as a clear conscience.
—French proverb

May I Remind You?

Dear friends, this is now my second letter to you. I have written both of them as reminders to stimulate you to wholesome thinking.

II PETER 3:1

Sometimes we need to be reminded of the things of God. We don't need to learn them all over again, just to be reminded from time to time. Repetition of God's truths will stimulate us to wholesome thinking.

My husband is a great reminder. When life throws me for a loop, I tend to overreact. I worry and fret and work myself up into a real dither. Lee is the opposite. He takes everything in stride. It drives me crazy! I go crying to him for some words of wisdom, some profound reassurance, or a stupendous solution to the problem, and what do I get? "It's going to be O.K., God is in control." Now what kind of answer is that? As if I didn't know that God is in control. I knew, I just forgot. God uses Lee to remind me—to stimulate me to wholesome thinking.

I will be starting a new Weigh Down™ session soon. The idea of watching the same videos and listening to the same audio tapes seemed boring (sorry, Gwen) until I realized that I need to be reminded of God's principles from time to time. Just like re-reading a portion of scripture will often reveal something new, I am sure that seeing the tapes again will uncover what I missed the first time.

Our minds are not capable of processing the vast amount of information we take in daily. We grasp the important points, but miss many of the details. Repetition is a great learning tool, whether you apply it to Weigh Down™ or the Word of God.

Today's Tip:

Listen closely to your Weigh Down™ tapes and videos. They will remind you of God's plan for eating. You might even want to take notes the second time through.

People need to be reminded more often than they need to be instructed.
—Samuel Johnson

Oasis

Here is a list of practical applications for you to try. Remember—these are not rules. The only "rule" you must follow is to listen to your body. Eat when you are hungry and stop when you are satisfied. But, until you get the hang of it, you might want to try some of the things that were helpful to me.

- Use a salad plate instead of a dinner plate.
- Resign from the Clean Plate Club—always leave some food on your plate, even if it's just a bite.
- Be a finicky eater. If it doesn't taste right, or look right, or hit the spot, don't eat it.
- Always pray before eating. Ask God to make it clear when to stop.
- Become a nibbler. Take teeny-tiny little bites and chew thoroughly.
- When you are finished eating, get away from the food or have someone get it away from you!
- Don't prepare your next bite before you have finished the one in your mouth.
- Stop *browsing* in the refrigerator and pantry. If you're not hungry—stay out of there!
- Eat a fistful of food! A normal size stomach is the size of a clenched fist. Don't eat more than that.
- Avoid "Eating And"—Eating and driving, television, reading, etc.
- Determine your craving. Do you want salty, sweet, sour, spicy, creamy, crunchy or chewy?
- Define your hunger—physical, emotional or spiritual. Choose the correct "fuel" to fill your tank.

Praise and Reflection

He satisfieth the longing soul,
and filleth the hungry soul with goodness.

Psalm 107:9

Satisfied

All my life long I had panted
For a drink from some cool spring
That I hoped would quench the burning
Of the thirst I felt within
Well of water, ever springing
Bread of life, so rich and free
Untold wealth that never faileth
My Redeemer is to me

CLARA T. WILLIAMS

Reflection

God's Word has practical applications for today.
Apply them to your life and you will be truly satisfied!

Celebrate Freedom

In Newness of Spirit

But now, by dying to what once bound us, we have been released from the law so that we serve in the new way of the spirit, and not in the old way of the written code.

ROMANS 7:6

I feel so free! Don't you? Just think, we never have to follow those written diet sheets again! We don't have to read labels, count calories, total up fat grams, measure our food, or plan menus days in advance. We don't have to buy fat-free, sugar-free, tasteless, nutritionless food ever again! We don't have to eat celery without peanut butter, potatoes without gravy, or salad without real bleu cheese dressing! No more diet cookbooks or endless hours of exercise or guilt over eating sweets or potato chips.

Today's Tip:

Make a list of the freedoms you have found through Weigh Down™. Now, compare them to the bondage that diets put you in. The cost of your freedom is obedience—is it worth the price?

We are free to ignore every diet guru on the tube and every well-meaning friend that gives us friendly eating advice. We are free to seek the face of God each morning, to walk in fellowship with Him, and to benefit from the blessings He bestows on those who obey Him.

This freedom is wonderful, but it is not without cost! There is a price to be paid for this much freedom, and that cost is the laying down of our will. We must set aside pleasing that stubborn little child inside of us that insists on getting his/her own way. But this is a small cost when compared with the total and absolute freedom that comes from eating God's way.

There are two freedoms—the false, where a man is free to do what he likes; and the true, where a man is free to do what he ought.
—Charles Kingsley

You Will Be Satisfied

Blessed are you who hunger now, for you will be satisfied.

LUKE 6:21A

I am so happy that God sprinkled the scriptures with verses just for us Weigh Down™ journeyers. I'm sure that was His purpose for adding a verse like this one in Luke, aren't you?

Hunger was one of my greatest fears, and yet this verse taught me that being hungry could be a great opportunity for God to bless me. The result is that, strange as it may seem, I am learning to enjoy being hungry. This is all new to me because I don't remember ever being hungry before Weigh Down™. That's because I never waited long enough between meals to really *get* hungry. I would just wander around grazing on snacks all day. If I thought I might be getting hungry, I would rush to the refrigerator as if hunger were some dread disease. On trips (even short ones) I always packed a cooler full of food just in case I got hungry on the way.

Today's Tip:

Take time to enjoy your hunger. Thank God for it. View it as an opportunity for God to satisfy you. Then go eat—but only until you are satisfied!

I kind of like being hungry now. When I am experiencing hunger, it's a sign that I have been obedient to the Lord. I have refrained from stuffing my face long enough for my body to function properly, as God intended it to function. If I don't eat until I am hungry, it's much easier for me to recognize that satisfied feeling. I have come to the conclusion that hunger is a blessing from the Lord, not something to be avoided, but something to rejoice in.

Now, please pass the mashed potatoes—I'm hungry, and I shall be satisfied!

Man's extremity is God's opportunity.
When we are quite empty the Lord will fill us.
—Charles Spurgeon

Dinner Invitations

If some unbeliever invites you to a meal and you want to go, eat whatever is put before you without raising questions of conscience.

I CORINTHIANS 10:27

Dinner with friends used to be a sticky situation in my old dieting days. I struggled: Should I tell the hostess that I am on a diet and can only have non-fat foods? Should I take my own food and risk offending her? What should I say when she presents the dessert and says, "I made this especially for you, I know how you love my cheesecake"? Weigh Down™ has eliminated this problem.

I am free to eat any food, as long as I am hungry. There are no restrictive rules to bother my hostess or embarrass me, because I am free to eat whatever is put before me. The only thing I must be sure of is that I am *hungry* when I eat.

This sometimes takes a bit of planning on my part. I may have to eat lighter at lunch or skip it altogether to assure that I will be hungry when my dinner is served. Sometimes, I will eat a few crackers if I get hungry before the dinner hour. By dinner, I am still hungry, but not so ravenous that I devour everything in sight before my body has time to register that it is full.

I can now go to a friend's home and enjoy whatever she has prepared for me with no restrictions. I am often delighted to find that God has planned a delicious meal for me. Eating it without guilt is the icing on the cake!

Today's Tip:

Use advanced planning to make sure you are hungry when going to a friend's house for dinner or out to eat. Then enjoy what is set before you with thanksgiving.

If we ponder to what end God created food, we shall find that He meant not only to provide for necessity but also for delight and good cheer.
—*John Calvin*

CELEBRATE FREEDOM

Don't Make a Spectacle

Be careful not to do your 'acts of righteousness' before men, to be seen by them. If you do, you will have no reward from your Father in heaven.
MATTHEW 6:1

It was so embarrassing! My health-nut friend was on yet another diet. We were looking at the menu and trying to decide what to have when the poor waitress innocently asked for our order. My friend had selected three possibilities from the menu and proceeded to drill the waitress with a tirade of questions about how the food was prepared. Was it fried or broiled? Did they serve it with non-fat dressing? Could they sauté it in water instead of oil? She proudly announced that she was on a diet and was a vegetarian.

After she finally made her choice, we chatted until our food was delivered. But even before the waitress placed the food on the table, my friend began to find fault with it. She returned the main entrée to the kitchen to be cooked a bit longer and refused to eat her side dish because she suspected they had used real butter on it. She reminded the waitress once again that she was on a diet.

My friend told me that the meal I had ordered was not a healthy one. Didn't I know about the chemicals they inject into beef these days? Was I aware of the fact that one should not mix a protein and a carbohydrate at the same meal? She noticed that I had used two creamers in my coffee and asked if I had any idea how much fat was in the creamer?

I was hungry, ordered exactly what I wanted, and stopped when I reached full. I had not made a spectacle of myself, and I had pleased God. Thank you, Lord, for this wonderful freedom.

Today's Tip:

Don't make a big deal out of your new way of eating. Let your actions speak louder than your words.

Where one man reads the Bible, a hundred read you and me.
—D.L. Moody

Guilt-Free Eating

If I take part in the meal with thankfulness, why am I denounced because of something I thank God for?

I Corinthians 10:30

Ah, lunch with the girls—what an experience! One sits, sipping her diet shake, while criticizing another, who is taking her appetite-suppressing pill. Another lectures her sister for ordering a steak and proclaims the virtues of vegetarianism. We would have had one more at our table, but she had to do her three-mile walk instead of eating lunch with us. The one to my right tries to convince me to stop all this Weigh Down™ nonsense and get on a "real" diet.

They just don't get it! God has blessed us with a wonderful variety of foods here on earth. He created it, pronounced it good, and invites us to enjoy. He perfectly designed our bodies to call us to dinner, and to tell us when enough is enough. We don't need the latest diet gimmicks to help us lose weight. All we need is God and a heart that is willing to submit to the will of the Father.

Today's Tip:

Resist the temptation to judge another for their food choices. Leave that to God.

It is with great thankfulness that I bow my head before each meal to ask God's blessing on His bounty. What a delight to be able to eat anything I want when I am hungry and to eat it guilt-free. If He does not denounce me for eating certain foods, I won't let others denounce me either. They can live by their food rules and regulations. I will live in the freedom God has given me—freedom tempered by obedience.

Perhaps as time goes by, the girls will notice that I am losing weight without all the rules and restrictions of man-made diets, and I will have the opportunity to share with them the wonderful freedom to be found in doing things God's way.

Men give advice; God gives guidance.
—Leonard Ravenhill

I Don't Have a Record

If you, O Lord, kept a record of sins, O Lord, who could stand? But with you there is forgiveness; therefore you are feared.

PSALM 130:3

Thank God. He doesn't keep a record of our sins once we have repented!

My senior year of high school, I fell in love with a boy from another school. These "long-distance" relationships can be tough on a girl. Everyday I would walk down the halls, watching couples holding hands, smooching and sharing their day. I'd clutch at his ring on the chain around my neck and want to hang myself by it. (I was a very dramatic teen.)

One day, I broke. I talked my best friend into skipping school with me to visit my guy at his school. We concocted some crazy story so his principal would let him out of school. We got busted! His principal saw right through us. He called our principal and then sent us high-tailing it back to our own school. Upon our arrival, Mr. Stone(face) announced, "This will go on your record!"

Today's Tip:

Let God wipe your record clean. Ask forgiveness for past sins.

I trembled. I just knew I would never be able to get a decent job. My reputation was shot! My record would haunt me forever. I didn't know that no one ever bothers to check those lousy school records!

God does not keep a record of our sins once we have asked for His forgiveness. He casts them into the deepest sea, never to be held against us again. It doesn't matter how many times you failed at weight loss. Repent for your failures, forget them, and go on to your success in God.

When God forgives He forgets. He buries our sins in the sea and puts a sign on the bank saying, "No Fishing Allowed."
—Corrie ten Boom

I'm a Pilgrim

Blessed are those whose strength is in you, who have set their hearts on pilgrimage.

PSALM 84:5

Just like those pilgrims in our American history books, I am bound for the new country. I'm not traveling alone in my pilgrimage, however. There are thousands of Weigh Down™ participants on board. We christened our sturdy ship "Lady Gwen" before leaving the harbor. She is named for the humble servant of God who told us of a land of promise and hope. She said that in this new land, we would be free from being controlled by food. Eagerly we began our journey.

Long we have sailed these ever changing seas. We have seen the gentle waves sparkle as jewels on a sunlit day when sailing was smooth and the wind was with us. We have spent days on a flat, deflated sea with nary a wind to fill our sails. We have drifted for days with no progress made. And we have clung to one another in the grips of a mighty storm which threatened to throw us off course and drag us to the bottom of the sea. But still we sail on, for God is at the helm—our sure and steady Captain.

Today's Tip:

If you are in the midst of the sea, have confidence in your Captain. He will deliver you safely to the other side!

We will reach the land of promise, and when we do, there will be much rejoicing. And after the rejoicing, we shall settle the new land, grow strong there, and spread the news to those still in the old country that there is a better way. There is a land of freedom from the tyranny of our past. We will tell them that we have landed not on Plymouth Rock, but on the Rock of Ages!

The faith of Christian believers is like that of pilgrims on a journey. They have to face many obstacles both within themselves and from society.
—*Tissa Balasuriya*

       CELEBRATE FREEDOM

Oasis

Jesus came to set the captives free. In the days to come, you will be experiencing greater freedom in your life than you could ever have imagined. Old chains of bondage will be broken as you allow God to set you free. You will be delivered from stubborn habits, wrong thinking, and slavery to sin.

Here are some areas of freedom for me.

- I'm enjoying the freedom of eating whatever food I desire. Even carrot cake!
- I am free from thinking I could never lose weight. I can, and I am!
- I have been set free from always trying to please others. I only have to please God!

Keep a record below of the areas of freedom you find as you walk with God each day.

Praise and Reflection

What doth the Lord require of thee . . . to walk humbly with thy God.

Micah 6:8

O for a Closer Walk with God

O for a closer walk with God
A calm and heavenly frame
A light to shine upon the road
That leads me to the Lamb
The dearest idol I have known
Whate'er that idol be
Help me to tear it from Thy throne
And worship only Thee

WILLIAM COWPER

Reflection

What are the idols you hold dear that keep you from a closer walk with God?
He longs to set you free—just ask!

Patience, Perseverance, & Plateaus

Hang In There

Let us not become weary in doing good, for at the proper time we will reap a harvest if we do not give up!

GALATIONS 6:9

A true sign of maturity is patience. Unfortunately, most overweight people do not possess a great deal of this commodity.

We want what we want, and we want it now—be it food or instant weight loss! We get angry and impatient when we can't eat huge mounds of food as we did in the past. We get aggravated if we are not hungry when it's time for everyone else to eat dinner. We want to throw our scale through a window when it only shows one pound of weight loss, when we thought for sure it would be five. Come on—admit it!

Today's Tip:

Make a list of all the benefits of obedience you have experienced so far, aside from lost weight. Thank God for these and review the list when you get impatient.

Try to be patient. Enjoy the fact that you are being obedient to God. Enjoy loose clothing, increased energy and inner peace. The weight will come off in due time. Until it does, don't miss out on all the other benefits God is bringing into your life. God will be growing you spiritually as He shrinks you physically. He always works on the most important things first. So, relax. I know you're in a hurry to be thin, but God has perfect timing—don't rush Him.

Don't use "false gods" (old dieting methods) to try to speed your desert process. Let God move you forward in His time to the Promised Land and a richer, more satisfying relationship with Him—not food. Change takes time, so sit back and relax while God does His spiritual and physical "makeover" on you. You're going to be beautiful, inside and out!

Our real blessings often appear to us in the shape of pains, losses, and disappointments; but let us have patience, and we soon shall see them in their proper figures.
—Joseph Addison

PATIENCE, PERSERVERANCE, & PLATEAUS

It's Only Temporary

So we fix our eyes not on what is seen, but on what is unseen. For what is seen is temporary, but what is unseen is eternal.

II CORINTHIANS 4:18

My eyes are fixed on the mirror. I want to be thin, and I want it now! I gaze into the mirror and frown. I have lost quite a bit of weight, but I still have too many rolls and lumps. I still look fat to anyone who did not know me before I started to lose weight. I still look fat to me! Will I ever look slim?

I don't get it! Just a few weeks ago I looked in the mirror and thought, "Wow! I'm really looking a lot thinner." I could see a big difference in my body shape, in the way my clothes fit, and even in my attitude. But, here I am in front of this mirror again feeling just like I did before I lost any weight. What's up?

I think I know what the problem is. I am more focused on losing weight to change my body than I am on eating right to please God. I think for a while I will ignore both the mirror and the scale. They cannot accurately measure the changes God is making in my heart.

Today's Tip:

If you find you are spending too much time in front of the mirror or on the scale, stop and consider whether you are focusing on the right things.

If I am submitting my eating to God, I can trust Him to change my body accordingly. What I see in the mirror right now is only temporary. The changes He is making within me are eternal because He's not just changing my weight, He's changing my heart. The obedience I learn during weight loss will have eternal effects on my relationship with God.

God saw not only what we were—He was faithful in seeing what we could become. He took away the curse of being and gave us the glorious blessing of becoming.
—A.W. Tozer

Don't Fret

Be still before the Lord and wait patiently for Him; do not fret when men succeed in their ways.

PSALM 37:7A

My friend and I started Weigh Down™ together. Right after we started, her family told her they were going on the Protein Diet. They urged her to join them, but she stood fast with Weigh Down™.

Week after week, her mother, father, and sisters lost weight at an incredible rate. My friend was losing weight, too, sometimes reaching a plateau for a week or two, but she kept on losing steadily. It was tempting for her to try their way, but one thing stopped her. She wanted to be able to show her family that God's ways are better than man's ways.

She remained faithful and lost 30 pounds in her first session of Weigh Down™. In her second session, she lost another 16 and is still going. Her family, on the other hand, has started gaining their weight back. Months of living on meats and fats set them up for a terrible craving for carbohydrates. Yes, man does not live on bread alone, but it's hard to live without it too! Depriving yourself of any certain food causes you to crave it. The cravings get so strong, they practically drive you to eat uncontrollably once you give in to them. At least that's the way it works with me!

God's ways are better than man's ways. Be patient and still before the Lord, and do not be enticed when the world offers you a "better way" to lose weight. There is no better way than God's way!

Today's Tip:

Make a list of the things that caused you to "go off" the diets of your past. Now, ask God to help you avoid those same pitfalls as you work through the Weigh Down™ program.

Great works are performed not by strength, but by perseverance.
—Samuel Johnson

The Tortoise and the Hare

The plans of the diligent lead to profit as surely as haste leads to poverty.

PROVERBS 21:5

You know the story of the tortoise and the hare in a race. The hare gets so far ahead of the plodding tortoise that he lays down to take a nap. While he is sleeping the steady tortoise passes him and wins the race. You just didn't know it was so biblical!

Are you the tortoise or the hare? Are you expecting to rush right into thinness or are you content to be diligent each day, moving one step forward steadily until you reach that finish line? In the past, I have been the hare. If a diet promised 10 pounds in 10 days, it sounded like a winner to me! But, dieting never taught me to persevere. As soon as I quit dieting, the weight came back.

Weigh Down™ is teaching me new eating habits. By listening to the clues my body sends me, I am learning a new skill that will keep my weight under control for the rest of my life. Far more important, though, is the lesson I am learning on how to live my life to please God. It takes time to teach an "old dog" new tricks, so I must daily take one step forward. I have learned that not all miracles are instantaneous. Some take time, but the results are just as miraculous!

I'll keep plodding along. I'll be content to move one step forward at a time. And, I'll pass up all those rabbits who are sprinting along on the latest diet craze. At some point they'll pause for a rest, and I'll be the one to cross the finish line! Are you with me?

Today's Tip:

Post a calendar and mark off the days as you "run the race." Remember: each day of obedience brings you one step closer to the finish line.

People testify about their search for the deeper Christian life and it sounds as though they would like to be able to get it in pill form.
—A.W. Tozer

Just Starting or Starting Over

Being confident of this, that He who began a good work in you will carry it on to completion until the day of Christ Jesus.

PHILIPPIANS 1:6

W hen God begins something He finishes it. I wish I could say the same about me. I am a great starter, but not too good at finishing what I start.

I used to have a craft business. I rented space in two local craft shops to sell my handiwork and also went to craft shows. I was always on the lookout for new craft ideas and supplies. When I decided on a new project, I would look for the best price on the supplies to increase my profit. Sometimes this meant buying in bulk. I'm sure you see where this is going. Because of my tendency not to complete what I start, I ended up with a surplus of supplies. I had *tons* of supplies that had to be sold at yard sales when I got out of the craft business.

This trait of not following through has plagued me all my life, especially when it came to losing weight, but lately, God has been showing me that I must complete what I begin. When it comes to eating right, once I begin, I must continue. When I fall, I must begin again. If I am to be like Him, I must continue any work I start and see it through to the finish. Therefore, I will keep on giving it my all. I will not give up.

Today's Tip:

Whether you are just starting or starting over, determine to finish what you have started.

Can you just imagine what would have happened if halfway through His mission here on earth, Jesus threw up His hands and said, "Father, I'm tired of this. Can we move on to something else?" I sure am grateful that He was finally able to announce, "It is finished!"

Lord, help me to begin to begin.
—George Whitefield

Though He Stumble, He Will Not Fall

The Lord delights in the way of the man whose steps He has made firm; though he stumble, he will not fall, for the Lord upholds him with His hand.

PSALM 37:23–24

What a comfort to know that it is the Lord Himself making our steps firm. He knows we will stumble, but He will not let us fall. This scripture promises that He will uphold us with His hand. That's great news for me, since I have never been very graceful!

I stumble. Yesterday it was with toast. The day before with pretzels. I don't walk perfectly before the Lord in my eating. I try, but still I stumble on occasion. Before Weigh Down™, however, I would have given up. I would have allowed my stumbling to become a fall. That would have been the end of my diet and the end of my hope to ever lose weight.

Today's Tip:

Make up your mind today to never, never quit! You will reach your goal.

God knows we will not be perfect in following Him, but of this one thing we can be sure. He is making our steps firmer as we go. He upholds us with His hand and will prevent our stumbles from becoming devastating falls if we allow Him to help us. Each time we allow Him to pick us up and set us back on our feet, we get stronger—we stumble less and less.

When you "blow it" with your eating, look to the Father to help you up, dust you off and set you on the road again. Be sure you let Him know that you are sorry for the stumble, for though we can blame a rock in the road for our stumble, that rock usually has rebellion written all over it. Repent, and go on.

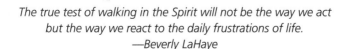

The true test of walking in the Spirit will not be the way we act but the way we react to the daily frustrations of life.
—Beverly LaHaye

So, You Want to Go Back to Egypt

But this one thing I do: Forgetting what is behind and straining toward what is ahead, I press on toward the goal to win the prize for which God has called me heavenward in Christ Jesus.

PHILIPPIANS 3:13B:14

Do you remember the song "So You Want to Go Back to Egypt" by Keith Green? It made fun of those grumbling, stumbling Israelites who complained about all the wonderful foods (leeks and garlic?) they had left behind in Egypt. They complained about their leaders, God, and anything else that came to mind. They seemed to quickly forget that they were slaves in Egypt! Rather than praising God for their freedom and looking forward to the Promised Land, they kept looking back.

Today's Tip:

Instead of looking back, look forward. Make a list of all the things you will enjoy once you enter the Promised Land of thinness.

All their complaining only angered God to the point that it lengthened the time they had to wander in the wilderness. I wonder how fast they might have reached the Promised Land, had they not kept looking back and complaining?

Set your sites on the Promised Land. Don't look back at all the foods you have been leaving behind. Nothing in our past has helped us attain long-term weight loss, so there is no point in looking back. Stop murmuring and complaining—it only prolongs your wilderness experience. Just press on with a good attitude toward the prize that is waiting for you.

That prize is "The Promised Land." It's a land of freedom from being fat and freedom from being controlled by food. It's the place we reach when we finally give our will to God and learn to be obedient to Him. It's a great place. Do you still want to go back to Egypt?

He ransomed Israel from the land of Egypt; He freed us from our slavery to the devil as He had freed Israel from the hand of Pharaoh.
—Melito of Sardis

Warning to Pay Attention

We must pay more careful attention, therefore, to what we have heard, so that we do not drift away.

Hebrews 2:1

When I first started Weigh Down™, I diligently listened to the audio tapes that came with my workbook. I took notes and concentrated on the message. When I went to the meetings, I paid close attention to the videos, noted the eating tips in the "café scenes" and looked up scriptures when I got home. I was losing weight at a steady rate, and I was happy.

Further into the program, I began to slip. I found myself too busy to listen to the tapes and sometimes talked during the videos. I still did my daily devotions and tried to stick with the proper eating guidelines, but I found myself eating when I was not really hungry and eating beyond satisfaction and sometimes right past full. My weight loss slowed down and eventually came to a standstill. I couldn't figure out what was wrong. (Duh!) Then I realized that I had stopped taking advantage of all the benefits of the Weigh Down™ program.

Today's Tip:

Set aside 15 to 30 minutes each day to work on the Weigh Down™ program. You won't be losing time. Each minute you spend studying is a minute you aren't eat-

The tapes and videos are chock full of tips and encouragement and valuable spiritual lessons. They will strengthen you while you are retraining yourself to eat God's way. Don't neglect all the tools God has provided for your success. Watch the videos, listen to the tapes, do your lesson, spend time with God, attend your meetings, and follow the guidelines for eating. Pay attention to the *full* Weigh Down™ message, and you will find that your progress is sure and steady.

When you meditate, imagine that Jesus Christ in person is about to talk to you about the most important thing in the world. Give Him your complete attention.
—François Fénelon

God's Timing

But do not forget this one thing, dear friends; With the Lord a day is like a thousand years, and a thousand years are like a day.

II PETER 3:8

God's timing is perfect—it's man who's confused. How many times have I thought the check should come in sooner, but God sent it just when I needed it most? How many times have I wanted to wait before making a move, but God had other plans? It's my timing that's messed up, not God's!

It's the same with my weight. I am so anxious to shed these pounds. I thought I would be at my goal weight by now. Seventy pounds in seven months seemed like a reasonable goal. Here I am in my seventh month of Weigh Down™ and I have only lost 35 pounds. I'm thrilled to be 35 pounds lighter, but I would have been ecstatic to be 70 pounds lighter by now!

Today's Tip:

If it seems to be taking too long for you to lose weight, sit down and write out anything you think might be hindering your progress. Commit these things to God and begin to work on them.

I don't know what the hold up is. On second thought, maybe I do know. I've been dragging my feet! I pick and choose the parts of the Weigh Down™ program that I like and follow those. But I drag my feet when it comes to the harder parts—the parts I don't like. I'm inconsistent in my obedience to God. I'm resisting the changes He wants to make in my heart. That's why it's been taking so long!

I guess it takes longer than I thought to teach a rebellious heart obedience. I just need to be patient and concentrate on cooperating with God more. I need to be content with God's timing for my weight loss. I just hope it doesn't take a thousand years!

It took me years to discover the premier lesson that God has a timing all His own and that I must not be impatient when His timing doesn't coincide with mine.
—David Wilkerson

PATIENCE, PERSERVERANCE, & PLATEAUS

It's the Little Things That Count

Whoever can be trusted with very little can also be trusted with much, and whoever is dishonest with very little will also be dishonest with much.

LUKE 16:10

Many times we look at the big picture. We look at the total amount of weight we have to lose, and whether that is 15 pounds or 150 pounds, it seems enormous. It can be overwhelming and almost keep us from even trying.

Think of it this way. Suppose you sat a one-year-old down and told her what the future held. You explain that soon she will be expected to master the complex English language, stop crawling around on her hands and knees and start to walk, then ride a bike, then drive a car. She will have to endure 13 to 20 years of schooling, then spend the rest of her life earning a living and raising a family. If that child could understand you, she would throw up her hands in futility and say, "It's too much! I can never achieve all that!" But she will do all that and more. One day she will look back and be amazed at how far she has come—one step at a time!

God does not focus on the big picture, as much as He does on the day-by-day, moment-to-moment decisions we are making, and that is exactly what we must do. Each time we say "no" to head-hunger, each time we wait for true hunger to eat, and each time we push away from the table when we have reached satisfaction will add up to victory in weight loss and victory in our Christian walk. A life of obedience to God is built on one act of submission on top of another. And finally, the big picture begins to look mighty good!

Today's Tip:

Make a list of the small steps you will make today, that will add up to a full day of obedience by this evening.

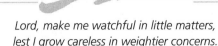

Lord, make me watchful in little matters,
lest I grow careless in weightier concerns.
—Charles Spurgeon

I'll Fly Away, Oh Glory

The length of our days is seventy years—or eighty, if we have the strength;
yet their span is about trouble and sorrow, for they quickly pass, and we fly
away.

PSALM 90:10

Seventy or eighty years old used to seem old to me, but now that I am more than halfway there, it's looking younger all the time!

It's funny how our perspective changes with age. As a child, the school year seemed endless to me, while the summer flew by. It took forever for my birthday to roll around, and now they rush by so fast, I can't keep up! When my daughter was a toddler, I couldn't wait till she walked, then talked, then started school. Then one day she was driving and dating, and before I knew it, she was married. Time flew!

Today's Tip:

Keep in mind that our struggle is but a momentary thing compared to the eternal benefits we will reap through obedience.

We have good times and bad times here on earth, and sometimes it's easy to focus on the trouble and sorrow of life. It seems an eternity when we are going through a hard spot in life. We wonder if we will ever see the end of the trouble and be happy again. If we could just realize how short our time here on earth is in comparison to eternity in heaven, we would not be so disheartened.

It's the same with losing weight. It's a struggle, but if we realize that there is light at the end of that tunnel, it would not seem so bad. We won't always struggle with food if we learn the true art of being obedient to God. Food will lose its pull, and we will spend the rest of our lives enjoying the food we eat, instead of feeling controlled by it. Soon we will be light enough to "fly away"!

The days of our life pass swiftly, as a dream, as a flower.
Why do we trouble ourselves over what is all in vain?
—Andrew of Crete

Oasis

As your body makes adjustments to your changing eating habits and your weight loss, it will pause to catch its breath. Don't let a plateau or slow weight loss discourage you. It is normal and necessary as your body shifts the fat you have stored into the "burning pot." Soon the scale will start moving again. Until it does—Practice Plateau Perseverance!

- Stay in the Word—Read your Bible and pray daily.
- Keep eating only when you are hungry and only until you are satisfied.
- Forget about the scale.
- Focus on other changes that God is making in your life.

Make a list of other areas of progress in your life, and thank God for them.

_____

_____

_____

_____

_____

_____

_____

Praise and Reflection

Now to you who believe, this stone is precious . . .

I Peter 2:7

He Is So Precious to Me

He stood at my heart's door
'mid sunshine and rain
And patiently waited
An entrance to gain
What shame that so long
He entreated in vain
For He is so precious to me.

CHARLES H. GABRIEL

Reflection

Aren't you glad that God is patient with us?
Let's practice patience and perseverance in serving Him.

Encouraging Examples

Group Encouragement

May the God who gives endurance and encouragement give you a spirit of unity among yourselves as you follow Christ Jesus, so that with one heart and mouth you may glorify the God and Father of our Lord Jesus Christ.

ROMANS 15:5–6

What a beautiful passage of scripture to adopt for our Weigh Down™ groups! The first declaration says that God gives us endurance and encouragement, the two most necessary characteristics needed for successful, long-term weight loss. Many of us have large amounts of weight to lose. It will indeed take endurance to see our goals accomplished, and there will be much need for encouragement along the way. Our Lord has promised to provide us with both!

The second thing this scripture promises is that God will give us a spirit of unity as we follow Him. Thank God for the diversity in our Weigh Down™ groups. They consist of people from different backgrounds, social classes, and church denominations. For this reason, there are many different opinions expressed during our time of sharing with each other. God blends all these differences into unity among us. This allows us to learn from each other, to support each other, and to develop life-long friendships with those in the group. What a wonderful blessing!

Today's Tip:

Thank God for the endurance, encouragement, and unity in your Weigh Down™ group.

Now look at the purpose God gives for providing endurance, encouragement and unity—"so that with one heart and mouth you may glorify the God and Father of our Lord Jesus Christ." As we allow God to take the excess weight off of us, others outside the group will notice and ask the source of our help. Let us glorify God with one heart and mouth and tell of God's way of weight loss to others.

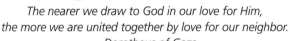

The nearer we draw to God in our love for Him,
the more we are united together by love for our neighbor.
—Dorotheus of Gaza

ENCOURAGING EXAMPLES

Mutually Encouraged

I long to see you so that I may impart to you some spiritual gift to make you strong—that is, that you and I may be mutually encouraged by each other's faith.

ROMANS 1:11–12

There's strength in numbers. Alone we may struggle, but with another to encourage us and hold us accountable, we can be strong.

My greatest help in this battle is the encouragement, prayers and sometimes the chastisement of others. My Weigh Down™ group meets each Thursday evening to share the victories and defeats of the previous week. I've learned a lot from the experiences of the others in my group.

My spirit soars as a sister shares her story of how God gave her strength to remain obedient at Wong's Chinese Buffet. My hope increases as another reports three more pounds erased from her body. My heart sings with joy as I hear the doctor's report that another's blood pressure is lowered and medication is no longer necessary.

Today's Tip:

Encourage someone today in their walk with the Lord, you too will be uplifted.

Even the negative reports of defeat serve to reinforce my determination to be obedient to God. I learn the tactics of the enemy and the pitfalls to avoid. As my friend shares the guilt she feels from a late night binge, I determine not to let that happen to me. Even when a group member forces me to face my disobedience, it hurts my feelings, but I am grateful my eyes have been opened.

There is strength in numbers. Go to your meetings with the intent to encourage your group members. Find a "Desert Buddy" to walk alongside you. The journey is long, but the road is made smoother with a traveling companion.

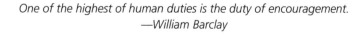

One of the highest of human duties is the duty of encouragement.
—William Barclay

Admonishment Can Encourage, Too

But encourage one another daily, as long as it is called Today, so that none of you may be hardened by sin's deceitfulness.

HEBREWS 3:13

Encouragement is critical to helping one another in our Christian walk. When we struggle with the daily challenges of living a Christian life in a sinful world, we can get discouraged. Just a kind word, a pat on the back, or a simple smile may be all it takes to lighten the load and help us to keep on keeping on.

There is another side to encouragement that is not as popular, but just as important. It's admonishment. Occasionally, a word of admonishment, delivered in the spirit of love is necessary to encourage others to be faithful to the call of God. For example, in my first session of Weigh Down™, some of the participants fell into the trap of excusing one another when they failed to eat in obedience to God. "It's O.K., it happens all the time" was the standard response when someone would confess to eating too much.

Finally someone found the courage to gently but firmly admonish us. It is not "O.K." to be disobedient to God. It is sin, and we must not let one another be hardened by sin's deceitfulness. We are not perfect. God knows that and provides forgiveness for sin, but He does not accept excuses for sin.

We were admonished, but we were also encouraged to be more obedient to God, to be more responsible for our own actions, and to be more accountable to one another in our group. Encouragement can take many forms, but it must always be delivered in love.

Today's Tip:

Encourage someone today to be faithful to God, and when necessary, love them enough to admonish them to keep them from being deceived by sin.

Whoever loves, allow themselves willingly to be corrected, without seeking excuses, in order to be freer to love.
—Hadewijch of Brabant

My Testimony Is Intact

. . . set an example for the believers in speech, in life, in love, in faith and in purity.

I TIMOTHY 4:12B

We had just finished dinner at our favorite restaurant and were heading for the door, when I heard someone call my name. It was my friend Nancy from my Weigh Down™ group and her husband Steve, seated at a nearby table.

We stopped to chat, and I realized that I had not one but two carryout containers in my hand. I had not been able to finish my dinner. God stopped me before I was halfway through the food on my plate. I struggled a bit, wanting to eat more, but decided obedience was best, and asked for a carryout container. There was too much food leftover for one, so I had to get a second.

I wondered if my friend would notice. She did. I was so glad that I had listened to the Lord when He told me I had eaten enough food. Not only did I benefit, but I was able to set a good example for my friend, who told me a few days later that she had not finished her dinner either that night!

Today's Tip:

Set a good example for others to follow. Keep your testimony intact!

It's important for us to set a good example for others. It's important that we show by our actions that we are trusting in God and in His power to see us through life. When others see us living out what we believe, they are encouraged to trust God for their own needs. Whether we know it or not, we are setting an example for others. What *kind* of an example we set is up to us.

Remember that God can use you to be an encouragement to others if you are obedient to His will—not just in your eating, but in all areas of life.

Be patterns, be examples.
—George Fox

They're Beginning to Ask

Because of the service by which you have proved yourselves, men will praise God for the obedience that accompanies your confession of the gospel of Christ, and for your generosity in sharing with them and with everyone else.

II Corinthians 9:13

It's starting to happen. People are beginning to ask about the Weigh Down™ program. The funny thing is that these are the same people who have made no comment up to this point about how much weight I have lost. I thought they hadn't even noticed. I even let myself get down in the dumps because they had not said anything. I was wrong; they had noticed!

I guess they were just waiting to see if the program worked. They were waiting to see if this was another one of my crazy diets, which I would abandon in just a few weeks. My perseverance has paid off. One of my big goals in losing weight was to be an example to others that God can help us through anything. The only way to prove that He is able to help with weight loss is to lose weight. The only way to lose weight is to stick with the plan. Perseverance!

If you think no one is watching, think again. They are watching and waiting and even hoping you will succeed, because if you do, they know there is hope for them. Stick with it. Hang in there. When you fall, get right back up and keep on walking. Not only will you reach your goal, but you will be able to show the way to others.

Today's Tip:

Remember, you are not just doing this for you. By your success, you will bring glory to God who is able to deliver us all.

There is only one influence that converts, and that is the example of a life which is shot through and through with the glory and strength of the spirit of Christ.
—Hugh Richard Laurie (Dick) Sheppard

Silence Their Ignorant Talk

For it is God's will that by doing good you should silence the ignorant talk of foolish men.

I PETER 2:15

It's amazing that one simple act of good can silence the ignorance of men. Several years ago there was a man in our town who lived in the woods of a nearby corporate park. Each day you could see him walking the streets in his tattered trench coat, carrying his meager belongings in a cardboard box under his arm.

One morning, my husband and I stopped at McDonald's for breakfast. We walked past a group of men in suits to find a table by the window. Just as I reached for my food, I noticed that homeless man through the window. He was washing his hair at a faucet on the side of the building.

My heart broke as the businessmen at the table behind us began laughing and making fun of him. I gathered my untouched breakfast and stepped outside. As I handed the food to the man, I said, "This meal is from Jesus who loves you very much." He grabbed it, mumbled something, stuffed it in his cardboard box, and rushed away.

There was total silence as I re-entered the restaurant. No more laughing or cruel remarks came from the neighboring table of businessmen. My action had silenced them.

In your Weigh Down™ journey, you may encounter people who laugh and make snide remarks about your new faith, good actions, and eating habits. Just do well—stay obedient to God, and you will silence the ignorance of foolish men.

Today's Tip:

The greatest proof to others that God's way of eating is the right way will be your success. Do what you know is good, and it will speak volumes to the foolishness of man.

*Blessed is he who does good to others
and desires not that others should do him good.*
—Giles of Assisi

Saying Grace

After He said this, He took some bread and gave thanks to God in front of them all. Then He broke it and began to eat.

ACTS 27:35

In this passage in Acts, the apostle Paul found himself aboard a ship that was about to be shipwrecked. He encouraged his shipmates to eat (maybe their last meal). But, before they ate, Paul took time to thank God for the food, in front of them all.

Do you take time to say grace before each meal? There is something special about taking the time before you eat to recognize that God is the source of all that you have and that He is the provider of even the food that you eat. Saying grace can be a testimony to others of God's provision. In our homes, it demonstrates to our family that we acknowledge God as our provider. In public, prayer before a meal may have an impact on others when we least expect it.

Today's Tip:

Take time before every meal to acknowledge and thank God for your food. It will help you, and you never know who will be watching.

My aunt and I were having lunch at a fast food restaurant one day. As usual, we bowed our heads to pray before we began eating. During our prayer, I heard a little girl at the next table ask her mother what we were doing. "They are thanking God for their food," the mother replied. "Can we do that?" asked the little girl. To the mother's credit, she said, "Yes we can," and they bowed and thanked God for their food.

The simple act of giving God thanks can do wonders. It can help you focus on eating to please God, on stopping when you have had enough, and on remembering that you must be obedient to God in your eating. Best of all, it may serve to remind someone else of the goodness of God.

Bless me, O Lord, and let my food strengthen me to serve thee.
—Isaac Watts

WWJ𝒟 with Food?

I have set you an example that you should do as I have done for you.
JOHN 13:15

Have you seen all the WWJD? (What Would Jesus Do?) stuff out now? It's everywhere—from the Christian bookstores to gas stations. I see it on two-year-olds with cherub faces, on 17-year-olds with punk hair, on grannies at the market, and on lifeguards at the pool.

I asked my nephew, who was sporting a braided necklace with the familiar WWJD? metal blocks, just what that means to him. He said it means that when you find yourself in a difficult situation, you should stop and ask yourself, "Now, what would Jesus do in this situation?" He was right, but he caused the old gears in my head to start turning. (That's scary!)

Is it enough just to contemplate what Jesus would do in any given situation? Isn't the whole point to take the same action that He would have taken? I wondered how many people who wear the WWJD? logo actually let it determine their behavior. And why do we only ask WWJD? in a *difficult* situation? Shouldn't we be imitators of Christ in *every* situation?

Today's Tip:

Ask yourself WWJD? in each eating situation you face today—then do what Jesus would do!

WWJD? with food? Would He spend most of His day thinking about it, preparing it, and consuming it? Just how would He act when faced with the all-you-can-eat buffet tables? Would He open the refrigerator door 25 times a day just to stare at the food inside? Would He fight for the biggest piece? Would He stash His favorite food in a secret hiding place to keep from sharing it? Hmmm . . . gives us lots to think about, right? But, let's not forget the most important thing—to actually DO what Jesus would do!

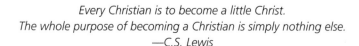

Every Christian is to become a little Christ.
The whole purpose of becoming a Christian is simply nothing else.
—C.S. Lewis

Teach Them to Obey

Therefore go and make disciples of all nations, baptizing them in the name of the Father and of the Son and of the Holy Spirit, and teaching them to obey everything I have commanded you . . .

MATTHEW 28:19–20

The last command that Jesus gave to His disciples included the instructions to *teach* people to obey everything Jesus had commanded. Obedience is key! Jesus was obedient to the Father's will, even unto death. He expects us to be obedient, and further, He expects us to teach others to be obedient.

How can we teach obedience to others? By example. Only when they see how obedience is played out in practical everyday lives, can people begin to see its importance and relevance. Only then will they be willing to learn from you.

Are you teaching your children the importance of obedience to God? By being obedient in the very basic area of the food we eat, we can instill in our children the value of a life of obedience. They will see obedience as essential for a happy life if they know that you value it so highly that you are willing to be obedient in even the most basic areas of life.

Fulfill the last command of Jesus. Teach those around you to obey the Father's will by demonstrating how it works in your life. People are watching you. What message are you sending?

We attain to true liberty, not by rejecting all authority, but by obedience, even to death.
—Louis Bouyer

ENCOURAGING EXAMPLES

Oasis

Setting a good example is the best way to encourage people to trust God. The word Christian means to be "Christ-like," to follow the example that Jesus set for us, and to be a model for others. Another way to encourage others to trust God is to uplift them. You uplift people when you let them know that you believe in them, that you are pulling for them, and that you are willing to help them achieve their goals.

I like to encourage by:

- Cards, phone calls, and pep talks.
- Eating right when I am with others.
- Being honest about my failures and showing how to handle them properly.

We should constantly be on the lookout for ways to encourage one another in our walks with God. Be sensitive to the needs of others and be quick to lend a hand. Make a list of ways you can encourage others. Record ways others have encouraged you. List persons who have been good examples to you and why their lives impressed you.

Praise and Reflection

I tell you the truth, whatever you did for one of the
least of these brothers of mine, you did for me.

Matthew 25:40

Help Somebody Today

Look all around you, find someone in need
Help somebody today!
Tho' it be little—a neighborly deed
Help somebody today!
Many are waiting a kind, loving word
Help somebody today!
You have a message, O let it be heard
Help somebody today!

BY CARRIE E. BRECK

Reflection

Be an encouragement and an example to those around you.

Crush the Rebellion

Don't Harden Your Heart

As has been said: "Today, if you hear His voice, do not harden your hearts as you did in the rebellion."

HEBREWS 3:15

Do you still hear the voice of God, or have you ignored it so many times that you no longer recognize it when He speaks?

In my late teens and early adult years, I was living a very ungodly life. I had been saved as a child but later decided that religion was something made up by adults to keep teens from having fun. So I went my own way. During this time God continued to speak to me, convicting me of my sins, urging me to return to Him. As time went by and I continued to ignore His callings, I heard them less and less. I had hardened my heart toward His voice.

Eventually, I saw the mess I had made of my life and returned to God. Once again, the lines of communication were open. I could hear the sweet voice of the Lord directing my footsteps, but how I regret the time of estrangement from my heavenly Father.

Have we become like that with our eating? When you first joined Weigh Down™, did you listen diligently for God to tell you when to eat, what to eat, and how much to eat? Have you started ignoring His voice in rebellion? Don't harden your heart, or someday you may not be able to hear His voice.

Today's Tip:

If you have allowed rebellion to creep back into your eating and have begun to ignore the voice of God, repent and reopen the lines of communication with the Father.

If we really know Christ as our Saviour our hearts are broken and cannot be hard, and we cannot refuse forgiveness.
—David Martyn Lloyd-Jones

CRUSH THE REBELLION

God Called Me a Cow

Hear this word, you cows of Bashan on Mt. Samaria . . . you women who oppress the poor and crush the needy and say to your husbands, "Bring us some drinks!" . . . Go to Bethel and sin; go to Gilgal and sin yet more... I gave you empty stomachs in every city and lack of bread in every town, yet you have not returned to me, declares the Lord.

AMOS 4:1–6

The other morning as I finished my Bible study, I prayed, "Lord, show me just one verse that will help me with my eating today." I let the Bible fall open and stabbed the page with my finger. It landed in Amos. (Who ever reads Amos?) I began to read.

Hear this word, you cows of Bashan on . . . "Hey, wait a minute, God" I said out loud. "You called me a cow?" There was no answer, so I kept reading . . . *you women who oppress the poor and crush the needy and say to your husbands, "Bring us some drinks!"* . . . Huh? I don't oppress or crush anyone! I do ask my husband to get me something to drink occasionally, but not that often. O.K., pretty often, but what's your point, Lord? I kept reading. Go to Bethel (McDonald's) and sin. Go to Gill (Dairy Queen) and sin yet more. Hmmm . . . I'm beginning to get it.

Today's Tip:

Ask God to give you a special verse for your journey through Weigh Down™. Remember to keep a sense of humor!

As I continued reading, the lights came on! These women (cows) of Basin were going through all the outward motions of serving God, yet they continued sinning. Am I like them? I say I'm submitting to God, but sometimes I still eat when I'm not hungry or eat more than I should. So, at these times, I must remind God of these women. At these times, I am a cow!

Most people would be offended at this. I was cracking up! God often teaches me with humor. That same day I bought the cutest little cow charm. Now I wear it on a chain around my neck to remind me not to be a cow!

God also has a sense of humor, an infinite one.
—Earnest Cardinal

Slow Motion

I will hasten and not delay to obey your commands.

PSALM 119:60

Doesn't it drive you crazy when you tell a child to do something and he takes forever to do it? When you tell him to turn the television set down, you want him to do it NOW. Instead, he sits there, pretending he didn't hear you, then eventually rises from the sofa, ambles over to the set, and turns the volume down a fraction. It's enough to make a parent scream!

My friend has a preschooler who is learning motor skills in class. They taught the children the concept of "slow motion" by having them move ever so slowly around the room while performing various tasks. That evening, my friend asked her son to pick up his toys before bed. He slowly rose to his feet, picked up a toy, and inched his way toward the toy box, moving with all the speed of a tired snail. "What are you doing?" his mother asked. "Slow motion, Mom," came his drawn out reply. I think my friend is going to have a long talk with the teacher!

How quick are we to obey God's commands to put the food away? Do we pretend at first that we don't hear Him and cram in those final bites? Do we do the very least we think we can get away with? Do we move in slow motion when the Lord speaks?

How nice it is when our children are quick to obey us. How wonderful to ask them to do something, and see them begin the task immediately, with no hesitation and no questions asked. We certainly appreciate that kind of behavior from our children and so does God.

Let us hasten and not delay to obey the commands of the Lord.

Today's Tip:

Honor God as your "heavenly parent" and obey Him swiftly and completely.

Holy obedience puts to shame all natural and selfish desires.
—Francis of Assisi

I've Already Blown It, So . . .

As a dog returns to its vomit, so a fool repeats his folly.

PROVERBS 26:11

Okay, so this is a pretty gross verse. But I didn't write it—God did. It's a graphic reminder that God considers disobedient people fools. Fools who keep returning to repeat their disobedient acts.

I don't know about you, but this lesson steps hard on my toes. (Kind of turns my stomach, too!) It's pretty embarrassing to admit that I am like that gross old dog, returning to eat time and time again. But, I am sure that is how God views my insistence in turning to food to meet my every need. Especially after all the times I said I wouldn't go back to my old eating habits. What a fool, to keep repeating my folly!

How many times have I looked at the clock on the wall and said, "Well, I've already blown it for today, so I guess I will have to start eating right tomorrow!" Then I continue to stuff myself for the rest of the day. With each bite, I am returning to repeat my disobedience.

What's wrong with starting right now? If my child was misbehaving all morning, I wouldn't want her to say, "Oh well, I've already blown it for today, so . . ." I would want her to realize her disobedience and behave for the rest of the day, wouldn't you?

So, why keep repeating your rebellious offenses to the Lord until the next day? Straighten up right now! Or as my Dad would say, "Straighten up and fly right!" Ask God to forgive your disobedience, do not put another bite of food into your mouth until you are truly hungry, and stop eating as soon as you are satisfied. Now, you're back on track!

Today's Tip:

Next time you find you have "blown it," don't give yourself permission to keep repeating your disobedience. Start immediately doing what you know is right.

Obedience is a little dog that leads the blind.
—Joseph of Cooperation

Perverted

"Then Saul, filled with the Holy Spirit, looked straight at Elymas and said, 'You are a child of the devil and an enemy of everything that is right! You are full of all kinds of deceit and trickery. Will you never stop perverting the right ways of the Lord?'"

ACTS 13: 9–10

Perversion is simply twisting something meant for good and using it for evil. Have you ever had someone take something you said and, in repeating it to someone else, twist it into something hateful, something you never intended to say?

This happened to Jesus repeatedly. The Pharisees and the Romans twisted every word He spoke. His words were meant to bring life and forgiveness to the world, yet they were twisted into supposed threats against God and the government until they did not bring life, but death — the death of Jesus Christ.

People so easily pervert God's creation. They take a drug that is meant to ease suffering and lure children into an addiction which destroys them. They take the beauty of intimacy meant for marriage and pervert it until it is nothing but a cheap imitation of love which brings them shame and disease. They take the Word of God and twist it to further their own false doctrines, leading many away from the truth. They take food meant to provide health and sustenance for the body and eat so much that the body is burdened and diseased from the excess. (Ouch, that one hurt!)

God's gifts to us are perfect when used for their rightful purposes. They bring life and health and beauty to all creation. Don't pervert the gifts of God. Use each gift for its intended purpose, nothing more, nothing less, and enjoy the blessings of God.

Today's Tip:

Thank God for the gift of food, and make sure you do not pervert the gift.

This is the definition of vice: the wrong use, in violation of the Lord's command, of what has been given us by God for a good purpose.
—Basil (Bishop of Caesurea in Cappodocia)

Out My Nostrils

Tell the people: "Consecrate yourselves in preparation for tomorrow, when you will eat meat. The Lord heard you when you wailed, 'If only we had meat to eat! We were better off in Egypt!' Now the Lord will give you meat, and you will eat it. You will not eat it for just one day, or two days, or five, ten or twenty days, but for a whole month—until it comes out of your nostrils and you loathe it—because you have rejected the Lord, who is among you, and have wailed before Him, saying, 'Why did we ever leave Egypt?'

NUMBERS 11:18–20

If you ever think you want to go back to your old eating habits, just read this passage and learn a lesson from those wailing Israelites.

Egypt meant bondage for the Israelites. They were slaves to the Egyptian people. God delivered them from slavery and promised them freedom and a land of their own. Yet, when they had barely left Egypt, they started wailing for the food they had left behind. They would rather have gone back into slavery than to do without the food!

Today's Tip:

Thinking of going back to Egypt? Think again!

God granted their wish for the food they left behind. He gave them a month's worth of meat. Nothing else, just meat. They ate so much meat for so long, that it came out their nostrils, and they learned to loathe it. I think I've eaten that much food! I've made myself totally sick on food! My stomach has ached and my bowels have rebelled! Come on, tell me you haven't been there!

I do not ever want to go back into bondage to food again. I will not wail to eat all the foods I ate then. I will trust God to feed me with His portion as He leads me through this desert to the Promised Land of freedom from slavery to food.

We are delivered from slavery at a great personal cost to the deliverer.
—H.A. Hodges

Purging Is a Good Thing

You must purge this evil from among you.

DEUTERONOMY 22:21B, 22B, 24B

This portion of scripture is not for the faint of heart! God was giving instructions to the children of Israel about dealing with sin in their midst. He was very specific about what punishment should accompany each crime. Most often the punishment included public humiliation, stoning to death, and a command to "Purge the evil from among you." Over and over He repeated, "Purge the evil from among you."

When God takes the time to repeat Himself, we should pay close attention. The point here is that God takes sin (rebellion against His will) very seriously! His judgment against it is swift and fearsome. Praise be to God that through his son He has provided us an escape from the terrible judgment of our rebellion. We can escape the awful sentence of sin by confession and repentance and accepting the sacrifice of His Son as payment for our sin.

Does that mean we are off the hook, so to speak? Absolutely not! Forgiveness is ours, but that is not a license to sin more. God wants us to "Purge the evil from within us." Notice, God calls sin evil. His attitude toward sin has not changed. Sin (rebellion) is evil and detestable in the sight of God and He expects us to purge it from our lives.

My eyes have been opened to the ugliness of my rebellion to God. Not just in the area of eating, but in any area in which I choose my will over His. It is an evil thing in the sight of God, and it must be purged from within me. To purge means to purify, cleanse, clear, and eliminate. This is what I must do with any rebellion I discover in my life. The first step is repentance. The second is obedience. I guess I had better get started!

Today's Tip:

Purge any rebellion from your life. Purging is a good thing!

Let us have clean hearts ready inside for the Lord Jesus,
that He will be glad to come in.
—Origen

A Willing Spirit Will Sustain You

Restore to me the joy of your salvation and grant me a willing spirit, to sustain me.

PSALM 51:12

The importance of a willing spirit is often overlooked. It will sustain you, while an unwilling spirit will rob you of joy.

When I was growing up, housework was *girl's* work. Since I was the only girl in my family, you can guess who had to help Mom with the housework. Each evening after dinner, you could find me standing at the kitchen sink, facing a huge stack of dirty dishes. Through the window over the sink, I jealously watched my brothers playing, as I slowly I washed each dish and seethed in anger. It's not fair, I reasoned. Just because I was a girl, I had to work while they had fun. I would stop to watch them play, hating each dish that waited to be washed. I usually took so long to doing the dishes that it was time to come in for the evening before I even got to go out. I was not a happy camper!

If I had just done the dishes with a willing spirit, I wouldn't have been so miserable. My chore would have been finished in no time and I would have been out there, playing in the yard with my brothers.

Today's Tip:

Cultivate a willing spirit toward God, and watch Him restore your joy.

Sometimes my unwilling spirit in the area of weight loss robs me of my joy, just like those dirty dishes did. I stand at the "window" and watch others eat lots of food. I pout and drag my feet at following the Lord's commands for eating. "Unfair!" my spirit cries. How foolish I am to make myself miserable with this kind of an attitude. If I would submit to God with a willing spirit, He would restore my joy as He takes these pounds off.

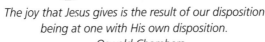

The joy that Jesus gives is the result of our disposition being at one with His own disposition.
—Oswald Chambers

Are You Listening? Is He?

"When I called, they did not listen; so when they called, I would not listen," says the Lord Almighty.

ZECHARIAH 7:13

We want the Lord to listen when we cry out to Him in prayer, but have we been listening to Him as He calls out to us?

Do we hear His voice over the roar of the Sunday afternoon football games, or the clamor of the music blasting from our stereos? When He calls us away from the television or the telephone, do we hear? Have we ignored His call to spend time with Him while we seek out the company of others?

God loves us with an eternal love! He provides for our every need and protects us from harm, and all He ever asks from us in return is our love. When our hearts are His, our ears are His. We hear His voice over the din of the world, and we walk obediently in it. Our actions follow our hearts, and our lives are pleasing to God. We cry out to Him in prayer, and He hears and answers.

But what if we are not listening to Him? What if we allow the voices of this world to fill our ears so that we cannot hear His voice calling us to walk in holiness? Then will His ears be so full of our sin that He cannot hear us when we call?

I am convinced that the only prayer God hears from a rebellious heart is the prayer of repentance. Then the ears are unstopped so that you can hear the voice of God and He can hear the voice of His child. Do you need to clean your ears?

Today's Tip:

Take a few minutes each day to shut out all the other voices that call to you and focus on listening for the voice of God. Then you will be sure to have His ear when you cry out to Him.

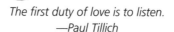

The first duty of love is to listen.
—Paul Tillich

Oasis

O.K., admit it. You're a rebel! You want to be in charge. You don't want anyone (including God?) to tell you what to do. Rebellion is at the heart of all disobedience. But, we can harness the power of our rebellious spirits to make them help us to lose weight.

Here are some rebellious activities I recommend.

- Refuse to eat! No matter who tells you to eat, or what they place in front of you, if you're not hungry, refuse to eat!
- Forget all those diet foods! Eat whatever you want to eat, but only when you're hungry and only until you're satisfied.
- Go ahead, ruin your dinner! If you're hungry at 3:00 p.m., eat! You can always join your family at the dinner table for conversation, but they can't make you eat if you're not hungry!
- Don't follow the crowd! If everyone around you decides to pig out, you do the opposite! Ignore the crowd and obey the Lord!

Rebels are strong people, but we can choose to use our rebellious natures to our advantage. List some other forms of "rebellion" that might help you lose weight.

_____

_____

_____

_____

Praise and Reflection

He . . . shall also quicken your mortal bodies by His Spirit.

Romans 8:11

Holy Spirit, Light Divine

Holy Spirit, Power divine
Cleanse this guilty heart of mine
Long hath sin without control
Held dominion o'er my soul
Holy Spirit, all divine
Dwell within this heart of mine
Cast down every idol throne
Reign supreme and reign alone

ANDREW REED

Reflection

Is God reigning alone in your heart, or are there idols on the throne?
Crush the Rebellion!

Food for Thought

God Heard Our Cries

The righteous cry out, and the Lord hears them; He delivers them from all their troubles.

PSALM 34:17

For years Christians have been crying out for an answer to obesity. We thought, if God in His infinite wisdom devised a plan to provide for our sin by sending His Son, surely He could devise a plan to rescue us from being overweight.

And He has. Weigh Down™ is the answer to conquering obesity. Did God put together a complex, hard-to-follow regimen of counting fractions of food, balancing nutrients, or using chemicals to help us control our urge to eat? Did He package it in a clever, eye-catching infomercial with famous stars to promote it? No. He provided a simple plan which is now sweeping the country by word of mouth because it works.

This plan is not really new. It can be found throughout the Word of God. In fact, it is the same plan He devised to deal with all our sin. It is submitting our stubborn will to the Father. It is acknowledging our weakness and depending on His strength. It is loving the Lord our God, with all our heart, with all our soul, and with all our mind. It's so basic that many stumble over its simplicity.

God has heard our cries and provided a way for us to overcome obesity. He has organized it through the Weigh Down™ program. He has drawn together those who struggle with overeating into support groups called the Weigh Down Workshops™. Everything is in place for our deliverance from overeating. Now the rest is up to us.

Today's Tip:

Thank God for supplying a way out of obesity. Follow His simple plan for eating.

With the goodness of God to desire our highest welfare, the wisdom of God to plan it, what do we lack? Surely we are the most favored of all creatures.
—A.W. Tozer

Food Is Not for the Heart

Food for the stomach and the stomach for food.

I CORINTHIANS 6:13A

We have become confused and have elevated food to a position it was never intended to fill. We experience, pain, heartache, depression, anxiety, or loneliness and try to ease it by eating food. We tried to make food fuel for our hearts. It's like trying to get your automobile to run properly on soda pop instead of gasoline—it just won't work. Not only will the car not run properly, but the wrong fuel will ruin the engine. We have just about ruined our bodies and our emotions by using the wrong fuel for the wrong purpose. This probably started before we became Christians, before we knew that God was the only one that could soothe the heart.

Now we are learning to use the proper fuel. God meets the needs of our hearts. Food can never provide what the Spirit of God was meant to provide. It's a cheap substitute and robs us of the true joy we experience when we turn to God to comfort our aching hearts. Feed your body with food and your heart with the Word of God.

Today's Tip:

Examine yourself when tempted to eat. Is your stomach calling for food, or is your heart calling for God?

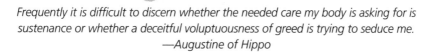

Frequently it is difficult to discern whether the needed care my body is asking for is sustenance or whether a deceitful voluptuousness of greed is trying to seduce me.
—Augustine of Hippo

Stress Eating

Come to me, all you who are weary and burdened, and I will give you rest.
MATTHEW 11:28

"I can't eat when I am upset." That always seemed like the most preposterous statement I had ever heard—a foreign concept. Why, the first thing I did when I was upset was head for food. There was comfort in food. I didn't have to think about my problems while devouring a gallon of ice cream. Apple pie reminded me of the comforts of home. Hot Chocolate soothed my nerves.

What was I thinking? Did the food ever solve even one of my problems? Did eating make them go away? No, all eating did was delay the moment when I would have to face the problem. It was a detour to facing myself squarely and dealing with life.

Today's Tip:

When you are stressed by life's problems, turn your anxieties over to God and let Him fill you with His peace. Food never solves any problem except hunger.

Not only did it not help; my problems compounded as I gained weight. I then had the everyday stresses of life *and* the excess pounds to deal with. I had trained myself to turn to food instead of God. I had replaced the One who could see me through tough times with a false comforter—food.

It's been a long road back, but guess what; I can't eat when I am upset! I have no desire to run to food during times of stress. I am too busy seeking the comfort and guidance of God to think about food. He gives me strength to get through my problems and peace as I work through them, so I am not stressed out. Food *never* did all that!

The better you become acquainted with God, the less tensions you feel and the more peace you possess.
—Charles L. Allen

182   FOOD FOR THOUGHT

Set the Mood

Better a dry crust with peace and quiet than a house full of feasting, with strife.

PROVERBS 17:1

What is the mood in your dining room during most meals? Is it rushed and hectic? Do you bring the worries and strife from your day to the table? Is dinnertime discipline time for your children? Stress tends to lead to overeating and often to a bad case of indigestion.

God's Word tells us that mealtimes are much more pleasant when they are peaceful and quiet. In fact, this verse in Proverbs indicates that the atmosphere during the meal is far more important than what is being served. Eating in peace and quiet doesn't mean, however, that we must eat in total silence. When the family is gathered around the table, it is an ideal time to catch up and to share.

Let's try something new. Let's set the mood for dinner tonight. Plan your meal so that you are not rushed and frazzled by the time you sit down to eat. Freshen yourself up before the meal. Play some soft music in the background. Take time for a peaceful, unhurried prayer of thanksgiving before the meal. Purposely keep your voice at a lowered, gentle tone as you dine.

You will be amazed at how relaxing a peaceful meal can be, how satisfying it is, and how much easier it is to control your eating.

Today's Tip:

Plan a "serene supper" soon. Set the mood and see how it affects your desire to overeat.

Drop thy still dews of quietness, Till all our strivings cease; Take from our souls the strain and stress, And let our ordered lives confess The beauty of thy peace.
—John Greenleaf Whittier

Stinkin' Thinkin'

. . . and we take captive every thought, to make it obedient to Christ.

II Corinthians 10:5b

$\mathcal{B}$race yourself. I'm going to give you a peek at the thoughts that ran around inside my head today. They're a perfect example of stinkin' thinkin'!

"I am just so proud of myself! I've been obedient to God. I didn't eat until I was hungry, and I didn't eat beyond full. I have been in the Word daily and have meditated on God's truths. I'm enjoying the wonderful fellowship obedience brings.

"I wonder how much weight I've lost? I haven't stepped on the scales at all in two weeks. Here goes! What? I have only lost one pound in two weeks? These scales must be broken! This program doesn't work! Weigh Down™ is just like all the other programs! Oh, and to think of all that food I passed up! God, I don't understand! Why aren't you rewarding me for all my hard work? And I thought I was doing so well. Now I'm depressed!"

Today's Tip:

Start memorizing scripture now to be ready to combat stinkin' thinkin'.

Whew, what a stench! Look how fast I went from positive thinking to stinkin' thinkin'. Negative thoughts quickly snowball and lead us into sin. Sin? Yes, sin. Allow these thoughts to run their course instead of squelching them, and the next thing you know, you've got an empty ice cream container, an aching tummy, and a guilty conscience.

How do we fight stinkin' thinkin'? With scripture! When you think, "I can't do this. It's too hard," say, "I can do all things through Christ!" (Philippians 4:13) When you think, "Nobody cares what I'm going through," say, "I cast all my care on Him, for He careth for me!" (I Peter 5:7) I think you get the picture. Stamp out stinkin' thinkin' today!

O God, sharpen my will. May it be like a sword
and cut all sinful thoughts out of my mind.
—Schenute

Ah, That Was Just Enough!

From the fruit of his mouth a man's stomach is filled; with the harvest from his lips he is satisfied.

PROVERBS 18:20

How I speak to myself makes a difference. If I continually tell myself I'm hungry, even when I am not, soon I will convince myself that I'm starving. If I say, "I can't have that, I'm on a diet," pretty soon I'm moping around, feeling deprived. On the other hand, if I say "Mmm, that was just enough," I find that I am truly satisfied. Do you see my point? Your words to yourself have a powerful effect on how you feel and what you believe. With the harvest from your lips, you are satisfied!

Often well-meaning friends or family will urge me to eat when I am not hungry. If I say, "No thanks, I'm on a diet," they continue to urge me to eat. But if I remember to say, "No, thank you, I am not hungry," they accept that. Many times I tell myself the same thing when my mind suggests that I eat when not hungry, and it works.

One of the more difficult parts of Weigh Down™ is knowing when to stop eating at a meal. I have learned to use the power of my words to help me in this area. When God lets me know I have had enough, instead of saying, "But, I'm still hungry," or "But, there is only a few bites left," I say, "Wow, I'm full!" or push my plate back and say "I've had enough, and I am totally satisfied."

Today's Tip:

Listen to yourself. What are you telling yourself? Are you encouraging yourself to eat right or do your words discourage you?

Recently I started to apply this truth to other areas of my life. I began speaking positively to myself—speaking truths from God's Word instead of negatively. It really does make a big difference in my outlook and in my actions. You should give it a try!

He that means as he speaks will surely do as he speaks.
—Richard Baxter

Don't Even Think About It

Rather, clothe yourselves with the Lord Jesus Christ, and do not think about how to gratify the desires of the sinful nature.

ROMANS 13:14

We are not to sit around thinking of ways to gratify the desires of the sinful nature. Too bad I didn't read this verse a few days ago. It would have saved me a terrible tummy ache!

Last night, I lay moaning in my bed. I was so miserable, so embarrassed, and so humiliated! My stomach ached from too much food. I had not felt that way in a long time. My eating habits have changed so much that I had forgotten what gluttony felt like. The amazing thing is that this whole episode started in my mind, not in my mouth!

Today's Tip:

Guard your thoughts. Don't dwell on thoughts of food. Instead, fill your mind with the Word of God.

I had been hungry for pizza for days. Now, there's nothing wrong with pizza. I can have it any time I am hungry, but I didn't do that. Instead, I thought about it (drooled over it) for days. Yesterday was a bad day for me. One thing after another hit me, until I found myself in a "blue funk." Then I thought of that pizza. It was late. I was depressed, and I ordered pizza. I ate way too much, and I suffered for it.

This is the exact pattern I used to follow before Weigh Down™. I denied myself the food I loved, but thought about it for days. Then just when I was weakest, I turned to that food to "make it all better." It would have been so much better if I had not sat around thinking of pizza all week, preparing myself to gratify the desires of my sinful nature. What was I thinking?

---

*The pleasure that a man seeks in gratifying his own desires
quickly turns to bitterness and leaves nothing behind it except regret
that he has not discovered the secret of true blessedness
and the way of holiness.*
—Isidore of Seville

FOOD FOR THOUGHT

Oasis

It's important to get to know your body. Pay special attention to the physical signals it sends you. Give some thought to the following questions and write the answers in the space below.

- Does your stomach burn or growl when you are hungry?
- Do you get light-headed and irritable when you need food?
- What signals does it send when you have had enough food?
- How does your body feel when you overeat?
- How long does your body like to wait between meals?
- Does the time between hunger signals vary with the type of foods you eat?
- How do hunger signals differ from thirst signals?

Today's Tip:

Praise and Reflection

I am the good shepherd . . . I lay down My life for the sheep.
John 10:14, 15

The King of Love My Shepherd Is

The King of love my Shepherd is
Whose goodness faileth never
I nothing lack if I am His
And He is mine forever.
Where streams of living water flow
My ransomed soul He leadeth
And where the verdant pastures grow
With food celestial feedeth.

HENRY W. BAKER

Reflection

What "celestial food" are you receiving from God?

Handling Holidays

Happy New Year

Therefore, if anyone is in Christ, he is a new creation; the old has gone, the new has come!

II Corinthians 7:7

Break out the horns and confetti, it's a brand new year! This is one of my favorite holidays. I love the excitement of the coming year. It's unblemished by mistakes and crisis and full of hope and promise. You can put the troubles of the previous year behind you and look forward to a brand new start.

Do you make resolutions? I used to. I would get a fresh steno pad, date it on the front, and turn to the first blank page. Here I would make a list of all the things I intended to do in the coming year. I think that "Lose Weight" was number one on the list for almost 20 years, followed closely by "Read the entire Bible from front to back." I meant to do both, but by mid-February, my resolve had dissolved!

I no longer make resolutions. It was too depressing to go back and look at all my failures written in my own hand, mocking me. Now I use that first page in my journal to list all the great things God did for me in the past year. It's a page of thanksgiving, a celebration of the goodness of God. Then, I rededicate myself in service to Him for the coming year. I don't tell Him what I want to do. Instead I make myself available for whatever He wants to do.

Today's Tip:

Start a journal! On the very first page, thank God for His care for you during the past year. Commit yourself to do His will during the coming year.

"Behold I make all things new." It seemed the one text in the Bible for me that day; for I was walking in a world indescribably beautified, indescribably lovely.
—Temple Gairdner

Be My Valentine

Dear friends, let us love one another, for love comes from God.

I John 7a

I am not very sentimental about love. Oh, I think love is a wonderful thing; I'm just not the mushy type. I don't believe love is something you fall into (like a ditch) or out of (like a bed). I believe it's a choice you make to devote yourself to someone for *life*. All that mushy hearts-and-flowers stuff is not me. I prefer the quiet strength of real love.

I do, however, enjoy Valentine's Day. It gives me another opportunity to let my husband know how much I appreciate him. He is so strong and steady. I can count on him through everything life throws at us. When a crisis hits, I'm running around like a chicken with its head cut off—ranting and raving, worrying and complaining. And there is Lee, calm and sure, steady as a rock, never wavering in his faith that God is in control and that things will work out. The most comforting place to be during a crisis is in the arms of this man of God.

Today's Tip:

Make God the "object of your affection." Make Him your Valentine.

I think that Lee perfectly reflects the love of our Heavenly Father. God is our rock, our refuge from life's storms. He is sure and steady and waiting for us to run into His arms when we are tossed about by waves of turmoil. There's peace in those arms and an assurance that God is in control and is working all things out for our good. What a perfect love! No mushy hearts and flowers, just a strong and solid assurance of His care for us.

It's this love that takes us through the "desert" in Weigh Down™. When our will rises up, threatening to throw us off the path of obedience, run into the arms of your Heavenly Father. He will pour His strength into your heart.

Christian Love, either towards God or towards man, is an affair of the will.
—C.S. Lewis

He Is Risen!

> They found the stone rolled away from the tomb, but when they entered, they did not find the body of the Lord Jesus.
>
> LUKE 24:2–3

*E*aster morn, and Jesus is alive! What a miracle! What cause for celebration! Because He lives, we have the promise of life after death, of victory after apparent failure. He has defeated the enemy of our souls and delivered us from the bondage of sin. Praise God!

I am sure Satan was shocked and horrified to hear that Jesus was alive. Satan had given it his best shot and thought he had destroyed the Savior of mankind. I am sure he was reveling in the belief that there was no longer any hope for the redemption of man. He likely thought that we would forever be within his evil clutches, unable to resist temptation and without hope that we could be rescued from sin. What a fool!

Jesus rose from that grave. He broke the chains of sin and death so that we might be free. Too often, we have allowed the enemy to blind us to the fact that we have been set free. He convinces us that we are helpless against the temptation of self-indulgence. He makes us think we can never lose weight. He is wrong! As long as we have free will to choose God's plan for our lives, the victory that Jesus assured us by His resurrection is ours for the taking!

Celebrate your freedom today. Celebrate the resurrected Christ, who purchased that freedom. Show Him your gratitude by serving Him in obedience.

Today's Tip:

As the sunrises this Easter morning, reflect on the risen Savior. If you already missed the sunrise this morning, there will be another one tomorrow—and Jesus will still be alive!

The great Easter truth is not that we are to live newly after death, but that we are to be new here and now by the power of the resurrection.
—Phillips Brooks

Independence Day

So, if the Son sets you free, you will be free indeed!

JOHN 8:36

Boy, do I have something to celebrate this Independence Day. I have declared my independence! I have been set free! Free from the tyranny of an awful master—Food. For too many years it controlled my life, but now I am free. Praise God!

Thanks to the Weigh Down™ message, God has given me the courage to fight my enemy and win. Who is the enemy? Food? Satan? No, it is my own stubborn will. Food is a blessing from God, and Satan has already been defeated, but my will has been ruling over me for too long. It has kept me under its oppressive control by constantly pulling me in the direction of my fleshly desires. No more. It's time to take action!

I have worked out a new strategy. I have harnessed the power of my will and used it to stubbornly obey the will of the Lord. I have used its power against itself and made it an effective weapon in the hands of God. My will no longer pulls me toward self-indulgence, because it is aimed at God, not self. I am focused on the target, and the target is doing the will of God. Food has lost its attraction for me. No longer do I fight what Gwen calls the magnetic pull of the refrigerator, for I am continually being drawn by the majestic splendor of God's love.

Today's Tip:

Cut a length of red, white and blue ribbon and use it for a book marker in your Bible to remind you of your independence in the Lord.

So break out the fireworks, beat the drum, and let the parade begin! I'm marching straight into the land of the free (free from food) and the home of the brave (brave enough to fight my own will). I'm going to declare the glorious freedom that comes with serving God. Anyone want to join this parade? Step right in line!

Dependence and freedom are incompatible.
— John Macmurray

Happy Birthday to Me

Before I was born the Lord called me, from my birth He has made mention of my name.

ISAIAH 49:1B

My birthday is almost here. You would think at my age, I wouldn't be so excited about one more birthday, but I am, because this year is different!

I will be thinner on this birthday than I have been in over 25 years. Let's see, how shall I celebrate? A shopping spree for new clothes? Much smaller ones of course. A mini-vacation? Someplace with lots of physical activities, now that I can move again. I'm so excited!

I think back to previous birthdays. I focused on the birthday cake and ice cream, a party with lots and lots of food, or dinner at a restaurant with a huge buffet. But all that seems so boring now. There really is more to life than food. I can't believe I just wrote that!

A birthday is a celebration of another year lived for God. I like to reflect on the previous year and look forward to the coming year. I ask myself: Did I do my best for Him in this year? Did I allow God to change me? Did I grow spiritually? What changes in my life will this next year bring? Will I be prepared for them? What great things will God help me to accomplish for Him?

Whatever the future holds, I know I'll be fine. God does not change. He will take care of me in the coming year just like He did in the past. I can rely on Him to guide my footsteps as long as I am looking to Him to lead me. Lead on, Lord!

Today's Tip:

This year on your birthday, think beyond the cake and ice cream. Consider what work God has for you to do in the coming year to further His kingdom.

As the Lord Jesus was made our flesh by being born,
so we too have been made His body by being born again.
—Pope Leo I

Harvest Time

The Lord will indeed give what is good, and our land will yield its harvest.
PSALM 85:12

Autumn in Ohio is harvest time and an exciting time of year. The leaves put on a display of scarlet and orange, there is a crisp snap in the air, the apple orchards are dripping with cider, and the county fairs are in full swing.

I love to visit the county fairs. I don't ride the rides. I don't trust anything that takes me hurling 60 feet above the ground at speeds faster than I drive my car. No, what I enjoy are the exhibits—what my daughter used to call the "old people stuff." So be it! There is something about a hand-stitched quilt with its intricate design and patchwork colors that speaks of how God takes the complexities of life and weaves them together to form a beautiful pattern. The rows of canned fruits and vegetables in their unclouded juices speak to me of the bountiful provision of the Lord. And the superior quality of the animals being shown by their young 4H owners, reminds me of the perfection of the sacrificial animals in Biblical days.

In past years, my favorite thing to do was to visit the food booths. I would wander from elephant ears to sausage sandwiches to mounds of homemade ice cream in a giant waffle cone. This year, I did things a bit differently. We ate dinner before going to the fair. I ate lightly to leave room for just one treat at the fair. I scouted the food booths to find the tastiest treat. To my surprise nothing really looked appealing! Then I realized I wasn't really hungry, so I skipped the food and had a great time at the fair!

Today's Tip:

This Fall, take time to gather your family close. Plan a family outing that will allow you to enjoy the simple things in life, like the county fair.

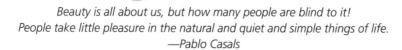

Beauty is all about us, but how many people are blind to it!
People take little pleasure in the natural and quiet and simple things of life.
—Pablo Casals

Trick or Treat

...in order that Satan might not outwit us. For we are not unaware of his schemes.

II CORINTHIANS 2:11

I've always had mixed feelings about Halloween, even before I became a Christian. I thought it was silly to have to dress up in those ridiculous costumes just to get some candy. But hey, a girl's gotta do what a girl's gotta do. If that meant dressing goofy—whatever! I wanted the treats!

There were six of us kids in my family, so the haul was pretty good. My parents had this wacky idea about mixing all the candy together, so that we could all have the same amount. Yeah, right! I was the oldest and I could cover a lot more ground than the little ones, so I always wondered why they should reap the benefits of my speed. To counteract that crazy "one for all and all for one" philosophy, I ate as much of my candy as I could before I got home. You couldn't outsmart me! Of course I was too sick for days to eat any more candy, but that didn't stop me from *wanting* to eat it, so I would sneak a bit each day from the "group bowl" and stash it in my room for when I recovered. My addiction to food goes way back!

Halloween still brings mixed emotions. I enjoy the memories of childhood trick or treat, but I am aware of the evil side of the holiday too, so I intend to take advantage of the holiday from now on. I'm going to pass out candy and Christian tracts that share the love of God with children, hoping that among all that munching, they will read the tract and find life's real treat—God!

Today's Tip:

Check out the cool Halloween tracts at your Christian bookstore and use this holiday as an opportunity to spread the good news.

A wise man will make more opportunities than he finds.
—Francis Bacon

What a Turkey

For everything God created is good, and nothing is to be rejected if it is received with thanksgiving.

I TIMOTHY 4:4

It's Thanksgiving, and here I sit reflecting on what a "turkey" I have been in the past. I thought of Thanksgiving as more of a sanctioned feeding frenzy, than as a time of reflecting on God's provision with a thankful heart.

Thanksgiving meant cousins, food, parades, food, naps, then more food! My mother and her sister married my dad and his brother. (Think about it; it's legal.) There were six kids in our family and four in theirs. Each Thanksgiving both families would come together for an entire day of feasting and fun. Mom and Aunt Nette spent the morning in the kitchen, while we kids sat in front of the television watching the Thanksgiving Day Parade and made frequent trips to the kitchen to ask if dinner was ready yet. By the time Santa waved from the last float, the house was filled with the aroma of turkey and dressing and fresh baked pies.

Today's Tip:

Don't be a "turkey" this Thanksgiving. Focus on the Provider, not the provision.

My cousin Butch and I had our own Thanksgiving tradition—a pumpkin pie eating contest. We kept it just between us, so we wouldn't get in trouble. We would see who could eat the most pieces of pumpkin pie before we turned green or got caught. Such gluttony!

I wish I could say that after I became a Christian my Thanksgiving focus changed, but I would be lying. I believe this will be the first Thanksgiving of my life spent in the true spirit of the day. Thank you God for Weigh Down™, which helped me to take my focus off food and put it on the Provider.

The world was made up of all kinds of good things, and gives sufficient indication of the great good in store for the one for whom all this was provided.
—Tertullian

Merry Christmas

Not that I am looking for a gift, but I am looking for what may be credited to your account.

PHILIPPIANS 4:17

Not that I am looking for a gift—Oh, yes I am! I love to snoop for my presents and to shake them and poke them, until I figure out what they are. Isn't that awful? This is why my family won't put my gifts under the tree until Christmas Eve. I tell them I've changed, but so far, they aren't buying it.

God knows how much I like to discover my gifts early, so He gave me an early Christmas gift this year. He gave me Weigh Down™. It's the perfect gift—just what I needed. How did He know?

I have been able to enjoy this gift throughout the entire year, and I haven't worn it out yet! Everything still works. I just have to follow all the directions that came with the program, and I'll lose weight! My body is in better shape than it has been in years. My relationship with God is on firm ground, and I am growing stronger spiritually every day. Thank you God for a great Christmas present and for not making me wait until December 25th to open it, like some people!

I have found that God delights in giving His children gifts and not just at Christmas time. His Word is full (just like a Christmas stocking) of gifts He would like to give us—health, peace, love, and joy just to name a few.

Sounds just like all those things we wish for on Christmas doesn't it?

I'm going to keep looking for gifts from God all year!

Today's Tip:

Share the gift of Weigh Down™ with a friend. Not only will it help him or her lose weight, it will revolutionize his or her walk with God.

There is an inescapable logic in the Christmas message;
we experience joy, quite simply, in self-surrender, in giving up our lives.
—Ladislaus Boros

Oasis

Holidays can be some of your most challenging eating situations. There's always an abundance of food and often types of foods that you don't get any other time of the year. Most people tend to over-indulge during the holidays, but it doesn't have to be that way. A little pre-planning can make your holidays joyful, guilt free occasions.

Here are some tips for handling holidays.

- You may want to skip your "lunch hunger" or eat something small at that time to leave room for an evening holiday party.
- Think about the foods that will be available at the holiday table. If you know there will be certain foods you love, determine to *sample* them in tiny amounts so you can enjoy all your favorites.
- Concentrate on the true meaning of the holiday, not the food!
- Use each social event to get reacquainted with friends and family rather than spend all your time hovering over the table.
- Wear form-fitting clothing. You won't be so tempted to over-eat if you are wearing a knock-out, slimming outfit.

Those are my favorite holiday helpers. Now, make a list of some additional things you can do to make the holidays more enjoyable and less of a temptation to over-indulge.

_____

_____

_____

_____

Praise and Reflection

Lo, I am with you always . . .
Matthew 28:20

Anywhere with Jesus

Anywhere with Jesus
I can safely go
Anywhere He leads me
In this world below
Anywhere without Him
Dearest joys would fade
Anywhere with Jesus
I am not afraid

JESSIE B. POUNDS

Reflection

We can take Jesus with us anywhere.
Let Him be your unseen companion at holiday celebrations.

Purely Praise

Stages of the Journey

Here are the stages in the journey of the Israelites when they came out of Egypt by divisions under the leadership of Moses and Aaron. At the Lord's command Moses recorded the stages in their journey. This is their journey by stages.

NUMBERS 33:1–2

Today's Tip:

Start a new section in your journal to record stages of your journey through weight loss or your Christian walk. Remember to praise God for the growth each stage brings

The Lord commanded Moses to record the stages of the Israelites' journey through the desert. It's easy to think of a journey in terms of the starting point and the destination—point A to point B. But, often the most important part of the journey is what happens *between* points A and B. The events along the way teach us endurance, build character, and give us reason to praise God.

My journey through Weigh Down™ and through Christianity in general has been marked by many stages in my personal growth. Each stage brought changes into my life—some exciting, some challenging, and some downright painful, but each stage was crucial to my progress.

I thought it important to share with you some of these stages, these milestones in my journey, because each one has given me a reason to praise God for the progress I have made. So, like Moses, I am recording some of the stages of my journey in hopes that it will cause you to reflect on your own journey, and to recognize these stages as reasons to praise God for helping you to grow spiritually.

In our journey towards God we proceed like those small birds whose flight is in loops. They always seem to be about to drop, but the drop in their flight seems to urge them forwards.
—Gerard W. Hughes

A Love Song

Praise the Lord. Sing to the Lord a new song, His praise in the assembly of the saints.

PSALM 149:1

I love to sing. I can't sing very well, but that never stopped me from cranking up the volume and singing along with my favorite songs. There is something about putting your feelings to music that lifts the soul.

Songs can take us back to a special time in our lives. When my daughter was five years old and we were living on our own, our song was "You and Me Against the World." When I had to take a job and leave her in day care, it was "Save All Your Kisses For Me." As I tucked her in bed each night, it was "Goodnight My Love." Even now we both get teary-eyed when we hear these songs.

I feel the same about songs that have ministered to me at pivotal times in my Christian walk. "You Are My Hiding Place" reminds me of a time when life seemed so awful that I would just run to God and hide myself in Him. "Have Yourself Committed" by Bryan Duncan cracks me up and reminds me of a time when God was requiring real commitment from me.

My favorite songs, though, are songs that swell from my heart during praise to God. They are songs that I make up and sing to God. The words don't rhyme and I sing off key, but they are beautiful just the same. I'm sure they are a sweet sound to God's ear, because they come from a heart that's "Hopelessly Devoted" to Him.

Today's Tip:

Write a special love song to the Lord, then sing it to Him. And "Don't worry that it's not good enough for anyone else to hear, just sing, sing your song!" (Karen Carpenter)

For that is spirituality—thinking, feeling, and acting in love, and singing praises to our Divine Lover. When we sing love songs we may use the classic scores of scripture or tradition, or we may make our own improvisations.
—Frances Young

The Swan and the Frog

. . . I reveal myself to him in visions, I speak to him in dreams.

NUMBERS 12:6

Years ago, my daughter Stacy was helping out in the office of the Christian school where she attended and I worked. A staff member stepped in and told Stacy that he had been praying and felt he had a message from God for her. (I was skeptical.) He said he had a vision of Stacy as a beautiful swan on a lake. Around the swan's neck was a chain, and each link spelled out the word "C-O-N-T-R-O-L." If the swan could break the chain, she would be free. Then he left.

Stacy and I were both in tears! This man did not know that Stacy collected swans or that she suffered from anorexia. Anorexics feel out of control and use their control over food to compensate. God spoke directly to my daughter's heart through this man's vision. It was the beginning of her healing from anorexia.

Today's Tip:

Praise God for the changes He makes in you through each stage of your walk with Him.

The next day, the man returned with a word from God for me! (I was excited.) He said he saw me "as a fat little frog, hopping about, spreading the joy of the Lord." Then he left. Whoa! Stacy is a beautiful swan, and I am a fat little frog? I glanced at Stacy. Through her laughter and tears, she said, "But Mom, you do spread joy wherever you go."

That day I began collecting frogs. Each time I look at my collection, I remember where I was back then and thank God for giving me that man's perspective on my life's path. I've heard of frogs becoming handsome princes, but I'm praising God for changing this "fat little frog" into a beautiful swan.

*I believe that we get a vision of God
when we are willing to accept what that vision does.*
—Elsie Chamberlain

204

One More Reason to Eat Right

Children's children are a crown to the aged, and parents are the pride of their children.

PROVERBS 17:6

I'm going to be a Grandma! Our daughter woke us with a phone call at 11:30 p.m. last night. We were thrilled to find out that we are going to be Grandparents for the first time!

After we hung up, Lee and I lay in bed grinning and talking until 1:30. We kept calling each other Grandma and Grandpa, just to hear the sound of it and then giggling like little kids. We were too excited to sleep, so we jumped out of bed, got dressed, and headed off to our 24-Hour Walmart store to do some baby shopping.

We raced back and forth from the baby department to the toy department, oohing and aahing over all the tiny baby clothes and cute toys. We wanted to tell our good news to the world! It was too late to call family members, so we cornered Walmart associates in the store and informed them we were going to be grandparents! They were very kind and didn't throw us out of the store.

Today's Tip:

Remember that your loved ones need you. Get healthy so you can enjoy life with them.

Again, I am facing a new stage in my life. Just when I was beginning to sing the blues over getting older, I find myself singing praises to God for blessing me with a grandchild! Now I have one more very important reason to lose this extra weight and get my body in shape. It takes a lot of energy to spoil grandchildren, and I fully intend to do just that!

Almighty God and heavenly Father, we thank you for the children which you have given us; give us also grace to train them in your faith, fear and love; that as they advance in years they may grow in grace, and may hereafter be found in the number of your elect children.
—John Cosin

He Had a Plan

For we are God's workmanship, created in Christ Jesus to do good works, which God prepared in advance for us to do.

EPHESIANS 2:10

It's amazing that before God created me, He prepared good works for me to do! I was no accident. God had works that needed to be done, so He created me with just the right talents and temperament to fit the job. Now, I make it a point to try and discover the works God has for me to do. I know that if I fail to see the work God wants me to do or refuse to do it, He can use someone else, but He wants to use *me*.

Recently, a deeply depressed young lady confided in me that she felt her life had no purpose. I shared this verse with her, and we discussed God's purposes for her. I could see the depression lift as she began to consider God's blueprint for her life. Thinking about this later, my heart leapt for joy! I knew that helping this troubled young girl was one of the unique works God had prepared in advance for me to do. I had fulfilled one of my purposes!

Today's Tip:

Ask God to show you the works He created you specifically to do.

Each stage of my life brings new works to do for God. One of these works is the book you're reading right now. I praise God for the opportunity to share my journey with you, and I pray that this book will encourage you to be all you can be in Christ!

A man should be encouraged to do what the Maker of him has intended by the making of him, according as the gifts have been bestowed on him for that purpose.
—Thomas Carlyle

PURELY PRAISE

The Great Love Affair

Love and faithfulness meet together; righteousness and peace kiss each other. Faithfulness springs forth from the earth, and righteousness looks down from heaven.

PSALM 85:10–11

There is a secret love affair going on between the faithful and their righteous God. Not everyone is aware of this passionate relationship or has entered into it, but for those of us that have discovered it, life is an exciting romance.

Faith flows from a people who have fallen in love with their Maker. They live their days to serve Him. Each morning they wake with His name on their lips and songs of adoration in their hearts. Daily, they consider ways to please their Love, and in return, the Righteous One pours out His love and blessing on them.

The fruit of this union is peace. Only when one is walking in perfect harmony along the paths of life with his or her true love can one experience true peace. When I am faithful to God with my eating, He kisses me with His righteousness and peace is born in my heart. What an exciting love affair! This truth so stirred my heart that I wrote this poem to God.

Today's Tip:

Write a poem to God, praising Him for the faith and support He's given you.

Faithful Sings to Righteousness

Oh sweet lover, righteous and true, bend thine ear to hear
Words of the faithful whispered to you, the one that I hold so dear
And pour out your peace, as soft as a kiss, on the cheek of your loving bride
And ever I'll sing endless praises to thee, as in your sweet love I abide
—JAN CHRISTIANSEN

I am praising God for this ever-deepening love I have for Him since I have learned to submit more fully to His will.

He who is filled with love is filled with God Himself.
—Augustine of Hippo

It Ain't Over 'til It's Over

I have fought the good fight, I have finished the race, I have kept the faith. Now there is in store for me the crown of righteousness, which the Lord, the righteous Judge, will award to me on that day—and not only to me, but also to all who have longed for his appearing.

II TIMOTHY 4:7–8

So, here we are! I have fought the good fight (most days). I have not finished the race and I still have more weight to lose, but I am confident that it will come off. In fact, I am looking forward to the rest of the journey. The first part of this adventure has been so much fun, I can't wait to see what God has in store for me as I make it down the home stretch!

Over the last few months, I have changed in so many ways, grown in so many ways, and bought so many new clothes. (Just kidding!) I wish I could tell you how wonderful it is to finally be free from the pull of food, but then, I know you understand just what I mean. I bet as you have journeyed with me you have soaked up a bit of that desert "Son." I bet you have already started applying the principles of eating God's way to your life and are seeing the results in the mirror.

Keep going. You are headed in the right direction. The Promised Land is just in sight. And as you press on toward your goal, remember I'm still with you. We will cross that finish line together and celebrate as we have never celebrated before!

Today's Tip:

Praise God for the progress you have made so far, then buckle up your sandals and set your sites on the finish line. I'll see you there!

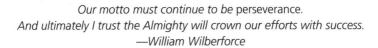

Our motto must continue to be perseverance.
And ultimately I trust the Almighty will crown our efforts with success.
—William Wilberforce

Oasis

In the coming days you are going to have plenty of reasons to praise the Lord. You will be looking better and feeling more energetic. You will have a new sense of control and accomplishment. You will see great spiritual growth taking place in your life. God will be pouring out blessings as you submit to Him. All these things are going to make you want to shout your praises to God.

I have found many wonderful ways to express my praise to God. Here are some of them.

- Write a poem to God about His goodness, His faithfulness, or the beauty of His creation.
- Write a love song to God or sing the Psalms to Him. Don't worry about your voice, He fine-tunes it on the way up!
- Begin a Thanksgiving Journal to God. Write in it each time you find something to be thankful for.
- Put on some lovely ballet music and dance before the Lord.
- Practice Silent Praise. Sit still before the Lord and praise Him from deep within your spirit, without making a sound.

These are my favorites. In the space below, why not jot down other ways you have discovered to express your praises to God.

Praise and Reflection

He lifted me out of the slimy pit, out of the mud and mire; he set my
feet on a rock and gave me a firm place to stand.

Psalm 40:2

He Lifted Me

He called me long before I heard
Before my sinful heart was stirred
But when I took Him at His word
Forgiv'n He lifted me.
Now on a higher plane I dwell
And with my soul I know 'tis well
Yet how or why, I cannot tell
He should have lifted me.

BY CHARLES H. GABRIEL

Reflection

God has lifted me out of the despair of gluttony!
Has He lifted you?

Books by Starburst Publishers®

(Parital listing—full listing available upon request)

More of Him, Less of Me • Jan Christiansen

Subtitled: *A Daybook of My Personal Insights, Inspirations and Mediations for the Weigh Down™ Diet.* In this daybook of inspiration, Christiansen shares her sometimes humorous, sometimes poignant struggles and triumphs while on this weight loss plan inspired by God. Her essays, reflections, tips, scripture, and hymns will encourage you on your weight loss journey, bring you to a deeper relationship with God, and help you improve any facet of your life. (hardcover) ISBN 1892016001 **$17.95**

Why Fret That God Stuff? • Edited by Kathy Collard Miller

Subtitled: *Stories of Encouragement to Help You Let Go and Let God Take Control of All Things in Your Life.* Occasionally, we all become overwhelmed by the everyday challenges of our lives: hectic schedules, our loved ones' needs, unexpected expenses, a sagging devotional life. Why Fret That God Stuff is the perfect beginning to finding joy and peace for the real world! (trade paper) ISBN 0914984500 **$12.95**

God's Abundance • Edited by Kathy Collard Miller

Subtitled: *365 Days to a More Meaningful Life.* This day-by-day inspirational is a collection of thoughts by leading Christian writers such as Patsy Clairmont, Jill Briscoe, Liz Curtis Higgs, and Naomi Rhode. *God's Abundance* is based on God's Word for a simpler, yet more abundant life. Learn to make all aspects of your life—personal, business, financial, relationships, even housework a "spiritual abundance of simplicity. (hardcover) ISBN 0914984977 **$19.95**

Promises of God's Abundance • Edited by Kathy Collard Miller

Subtitled: *For a More Meaningful Life.* The Bible is filled with God's promises for an abundant life. *Promises of God's Abundance for a More Meaningful Life* is written in the same way as the best-selling *God's Abundance.* It will help you discover these promises and show you how simple obedience is the key to an abundant life. Scripture, questions for growth and a simple thought for the day will guide you to a more meaningful life. ISBN 0914984098 **$9.95**

God's Unexpected Blessings • Edited by Kathy Collard Miller

Subtitled: *What to Expect from God When You Least Expect It.* Learn to see the *Unexpected Blessings* in life. These individual essays describe experiences that seem negative on the surface but are something God has used for good in our lives or to benefit others. Witness God at work in our lives. Learn to trust God in action. Realize that we always have a choice to learn and benefit from these experiences by letting God prove His promise of turning all things for our good. (hardcover) ISBN 0914984071 **$18.95**

A Woman's Guide To Spiritual Power • Nancy L. Dorner

Subtitled: *Through Scriptural Prayer.* Do your prayers seem to go "against a brick wall"? Does God sometimes seem far away or non-existent? If your answer is "Yes," you are not alone. Prayer must be the cornerstone of your relationship to God. "This book is a powerful tool for anyone who is serious about prayer and discipleship."—Florence Littauer. (trade paper)   ISBN 0914984470   **$9.95**

God's Vitamin "C" for the Spirit • Kathy Collard Miller & D. Larry Miller

Subtitled: *"Tug-at-the-Heart" Stories to Fortify and Enrich Your Life.* Includes inspiring stories and anecdotes that emphasize Christian ideals and values by Barbara Johnson, Billy Graham, Nancy L. Dorner, and many other well-known Christian speakers and writers. Topics include: Love, Family Life, Faith and Trust, Prayer, and God's Guidance. (trade paper)   ISBN 0914984837   **$12.95**

God's Vitamin "C" for the Spirit of WOMEN • Kathy Collard Miller

Subtitled: *"Tug-at-the-Heart" Stories to Inspire and Delight Your Spirit.* A beautiful treasury of timeless stories, quotes, and poetry designed by and for women. Well-known Christian women like Liz Curtis Higgs, Patsy Clairmont, Naomi Rhode, and Elisabeth Elliott share from their hearts on subjects like Marriage, Motherhood, Christian Living, Faith, and Friendship.   (trade paper)   ISBN 0914984934   **$12.95**

God's Chewable Vitamin "C" for the Spirit of MOMs

Delightful, Insightful, and Inspirational quotes combined with Scripture that uplift and encourage women to succeed at the most important job in life—Motherhood. (trade paper)   ISBN 0914984942   **$6.95**

The Frazzled Working Woman's Practical Guide to Motherhood • Mary Lyon

It's Erma Bombeck meets Martha Stewart meets cartoonist Cathy Guisewite! Mary Lyon's extensive, original cartoon illustrations enliven this sparklingly humorous narrative, making Lyon a new James Thurber! *Frazzled* is an essential companion for any working woman who thinks she wants a baby or is currently expecting one—especially if she could use a good laugh to lighten her load and her worries. This book also offers an innovative update on effective working-mom strategies to women who are already off and running on the "Mommy Track."   (trade paper)   ISBN 0914984756   **$14.95**

The Fragile Thread • Aliske Webb

Aliske Webb, bestselling author of *Twelve Golden Threads*, depicts a touching story that traces a woman's journey of transformation. After burying a husband and raising three children, Aggie reaches mid-life alone and makes a major decision: to move to a small town and open a quilt shop. In the process, she discovers the importance of community and rediscovers her values, beliefs and spiritual foundation. (hardcover)   ISBN 0914984543   **$17.95**

Women of the Bible—God's Word for the Biblically-Inept™ • Kathy Collard Miller

Shows that although the Bible was written many years ago, it is still relevant for today. Gain valuable insight from the successes and struggles of women such as Eve, Esther, Mary, Sarah, and Rebekah. Comments from leading experts will make learning about God's Word easy to understand and incorporate into your daily life.
(trade paper)   ISBN 0914984063   **$16.95**

The Bible—God's Word for the Biblically-Inept™ • Larry Richards

A Bible overview that makes the Bible easy to understand. Each chapter contains select verses from books of the Bible along with illustrations, definitions, and references to related Bible passages. It's the Bible made easy!
(trade paper)   ISBN 0914984551   **$16.95**

Health and Nutrition—God's Word for the Biblically-Inept™
Kathleen O'Bannon Baldinger
Gives scientific evidence that proves that the diet and health principles outlined in the Bible are the best diet for total health. Experts include Pamela Smith, Julian Whitaker, Kenneth Cooper, and TD Jakes.
(trade paper)   ISBN 0914984055   **$16.95**

If I Only Knew . . . What Would Jesus Do? • Joan Hake Robie

Finally, a WWJD? for adults! This book looks at dozens of everyday problems through the lens of the fundamental teachings of Jesus.
(trade paper)   ISBN 091498439X   **$16.95**

If I Only Knew . . . What Would Jesus Do?—For Women • Joan Hake Robie

In the same helpful manner as the first *If I Only Knew . . . What Would Jesus Do?*, this book is packed with Jesus' perspective on the everyday struggles that only women face. A must read for any woman wishing to live a spirit-filled life.
(trade paper)   ISBN 1892016087   **$9.95**